D0827929

ASAP

European History

By the Staff of The Princeton Review

princetonreview.com

Penguin
Random
House

The Princeton Review
110 East 42nd Street, 7th Floor
New York, NY 10017
Email: editorialsupport@review.com

Copyright © 2018 by TPR Education IP
Holdings, LLC. All rights reserved.

Published in the United States by Penguin
Random House LLC, New York, and in Canada
by Random House of Canada, a division of
Penguin Random House Ltd., Toronto.

Terms of Service: The Princeton Review Online
Companion Tools ("Student Tools") for retail
books are available for only the two most recent
editions of that book. Student Tools may be
activated only twice per eligible book purchased
for two consecutive 12-month periods, for a
total of 24 months of access. Activation of
Student Tools more than twice per book is in
direct violation of these Terms of Service and
may result in discontinuation of access to
Student Tools Services.

ISBN: 978-0-525-56769-1
eBook ISBN: 978-0-525-56780-6
ISSN: 2576-6848

AP is a trademark registered and owned by the
College Board, which is not affiliated with, and
does not endorse, this product.

The Princeton Review is not affiliated with
Princeton University.

Editor: Sarah Litt
Production Editors: Jim Melloan and
                   Kathy Carter
Production Artist: Deborah A. Weber

Printed in the United States of America.

10 9 8 7 6 5 4 3 2 1

Editorial

Rob Franek, Editor-in-Chief
Mary Beth Garrick, Executive Director of Production
Craig Patches, Production Design Manager
Selena Coppock, Managing Editor
Meave Shelton, Senior Editor
Colleen Day, Editor
Sarah Litt, Editor
Aaron Riccio, Editor
Orion McBean, Associate Editor

Penguin Random House Publishing Team

Tom Russell, VP, Publisher
Alison Stoltzfus, Publishing Director
Amanda Yee, Associate Managing Editor
Ellen Reed, Production Manager
Suzanne Lee, Designer

Acknowledgments

The Princeton Review would like to thank everyone who worked so hard on this book.

Our fantastic content team researched and helped create the book in your hands: Kevin Kelly, Jason Morgan, and John D. Robertson.

Our terrific production artists, Deborah Weber and Craig Patches, created many of the images throughout the book and the entirety of the layout and design. The book wouldn't look nearly as wonderful were it not for their talent.

Our intrepid Production Editors, Jim Melloan and Kathy Carter reviewed this book to make sure all the facts are as they should be—and made sure everyone's names were spelled correctly!

Contents

Get More (Free) Content

1 Go to **PrincetonReview.com/cracking.**

2 Enter the following ISBN for your book: 9780525567691.

3 Answer a few simple questions to set up an exclusive Princeton Review account. (If you already have one, you can just log in.)

4 Click the "Student Tools" button, also found under "My Account" from the top toolbar. You're all set to access your bonus content!

Need to report a potential **content** issue?

Contact **EditorialSupport@review.com**.

Include:

- full title of the book
- ISBN
- page number

Need to report a **technical** issue?

Contact **TPRStudentTech@review.com** and provide:

- your full name
- email address used to register the book
- full book title and ISBN
- computer OS (Mac/PC) and browser (Firefox, Safari, etc.)

The Princeton Review®

Once you've registered, you can...

- Get valuable advice about the college application process, including tips for writing a great essay and where to apply for financial aid

- If you're still choosing between colleges, use our searchable rankings of *The Best 384 Colleges* to find out more information about your dream school

- Check to see if there have been any corrections or updates to this edition

- Get our take on any recent or pending updates to the AP European History Exam

Introduction

What Is This Book and When Should I Use It?

Welcome to *ASAP European History,* written by the Staff of The Princeton Review to serve as a quick-review study guide for the AP Exam. This is a brand-new series custom-built for crammers, visual learners, and any student doing high-level AP concept review. As you read through this book, you will notice that there aren't any practice tests, end-of-chapter drills, or multiple-choice questions. There's also very little test-taking strategy presented in here. Both of those things (practice and strategy) can be found in The Princeton Review's other top-notch AP series—*Cracking*. So if you need a deep dive into AP European History, check out *Cracking the AP European History Exam* at your local bookstore or online.

ASAP European History is our fast track to understanding the material—like a fantastic set of class notes. We present the most important information that you MUST know (or should know or could know—more on that later) in visually friendly formats such as charts, graphs, and maps, and we even threw in a few jokes to keep things interesting.

Use this book any time you want—it's never too late to do some studying (nor is it ever too early). It's small, so you can take it with you anywhere and crack it open while you're waiting for soccer practice to start, for your friend to meet you for a study date, or for the library to open.* *ASAP European History* is the perfect study guide for students who need high-level review in addition to their regular review and also for students who perhaps need to cram pre-Exam. Whatever you need it for, you'll find no judgment here!

 *Because you camp out in front of the library like they are selling concert tickets in there, right?

Who Is This Book For?

This book is for YOU! No matter what kind of student you are, this book is the right one for you. How do you know what kind of student you are? Follow this handy chart to find out!

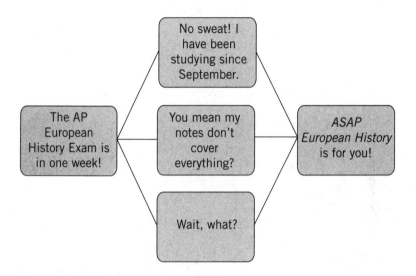

As you can see, this book is meant for every kind of student. Our quick lessons let you focus on the topics you must know, you should know, and you could know—that way, even if the test is tomorrow (!), you can get a little extra study time in, and learn only the material you need.

How Do I Use This Book?

This book is your study tool, so feel free to customize it in whatever way makes the most sense to you, given your available time to prepare. Here are some suggestions:

Target Practice

If you know what topics give you the most trouble, hone in on those chapters or sections.

ASK Away

Answer all of the ASK questions *first*. This will help you to identify any additional tough spots that may need special attention.

Three-Pass System

Start at the very beginning!* Read the book several times from cover to cover, focusing selectively on the MUST content for your first pass, the SHOULD content for your second pass, and finally, the COULD content.

 *It's a very good place to start.

Why Are There Icons?

Your standard AP course is designed to be equivalent to a college-level class, and as such, the amount of material that's covered may seem overwhelming. It's certainly admirable to want to learn everything—these are, after all, fascinating subjects. But every student's course load, to say nothing of his or her life, is different, and there isn't always time to memorize every last fact.

To that end, *ASAP European History* doesn't just distill the key information into bite-sized chunks and memorable tables and figures. This book also breaks down the material into three major types of content:

❗ This symbol calls out a section that has MUST KNOW information. This is the core content that is either the most likely to appear in some format on the test or is foundational knowledge that's needed to make sense of other highly tested topics.

💬 This symbol refers to SHOULD KNOW material. This is either content that has been tested in some form before (but not as frequently) or which will help you to deepen your understanding of the surrounding topics. If you're pressed for time, you might just want to skim it, and read only those sections that you feel particularly unfamiliar with.

〰 This symbol indicates COULD KNOW material, but don't just write it off! This material is still within the AP's expansive curriculum, so if you're aiming for a perfect 5, you should still know all of this. That said, this is the information that is least likely to be directly tested, so if the test is just around the corner, you should probably save this material for last.

As you work through the book, you'll also notice a few other types of icons.

The Ask Yourself question is an opportunity to solidify your understanding of the material you've just read. It's also a great way to take these concepts outside of the book and make the sort of real-world connections that you'll need in order to answer the free-response questions on the AP Exam.

There's a reason why people say that "All work and no play" is a bad thing. These jokes help to shake your brain up a bit and keep it from just glazing over all of the content—they're a bit like mental speed bumps, there to keep you from going too fast for your own good.

There's a lot to think about in this book, and when you see this guy, know that the information that follows is always good to have on hand. You'll rock it in trivia, if no place else.

Where Can I Find Other Resources?

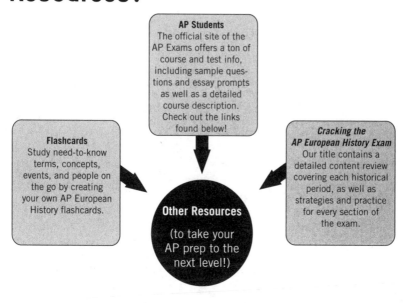

AP Students
The official site of the AP Exams offers a ton of course and test info, including sample questions and essay prompts as well as a detailed course description. Check out the links found below!

Flashcards
Study need-to-know terms, concepts, events, and people on the go by creating your own AP European History flashcards.

Cracking the AP European History Exam
Our title contains a detailed content review covering each historical period, as well as strategies and practice for every section of the exam.

Other Resources
(to take your AP prep to the next level!)

Useful Links

- AP European History Homepage: https://apstudent.collegeboard.org/apcourse/ap-european-history
- Your Student Tools: www.PrincetonReview.com/cracking
  See the "Get More (Free) Content" page for step-by-step instructions for registering your book and accessing more materials to boost your test prep.

CHAPTER 1

The Renaissance to Wars of Religion: c. 1450–c. 1648

Overview ❗

The Renaissance was a rebirth of culture, arts, and thought that occurred on the Italian peninsula starting in the late 15th century. It later spread to northern Europe.

Background: Western Europe, despite its modern reputation for carefully tended ruins, was not particularly good at taking care of its own treasures over the centuries. During the Dark Ages, Europeans often lost valuable things—in particular, the works of their ancient thinkers and philosophers. By the late medieval period, many works by Aristotle, Plato, and others had disappeared.

Then the 15th century arrived. The urban Italian middle class started to make contact with Arabic traders from the eastern Mediterranean. They discovered that the Arabs had preserved the works of many of those thinkers, translated into Arabic! Likewise, the Fall of Constantinople in 1453 sent many Greek scholars fleeing Greece and into Italy—carrying with them even more lost texts back to Western Europe.

All this newly rediscovered knowledge opened up the Italian peninsula —and eventually Western Europe—to classical ideas such as **individualism**. This idea in particular had been forgotten for the previous thousand years that Europe had spent under the thumb of the medieval Catholic Church.

Italian City-States ❗

Like many other regions of Europe in the 15th and 16th centuries, Italy was *not* a unified nation. It was a loose collection of rival city-states which were constantly forming alliances and breaking them.*

---

 *Unlike many other regions in Europe, however, Italy remained divided into city-states, all the way until 1870s! And some even argue that Italy never truly unified, especially if you've ever heard two Italians argue about food.

Of the 15 city-states, the three most powerful were **Milan, Florence, and Venice**. They became de facto regional capitals and were pioneers in banking, manufacturing, education, and maritime power. In fact, the birth of the modern European middle class began in these sity-states, largely because they were the first to make "the exit from feudalism," in the words of one visiting German scholar.* The Papal states in the middle of the peninsula, though dominated by the pope and the seat of the Catholic Church, were weak and poorly administered. To the south, the Kingdom of the Two Sicilies was both the largest and poorest.

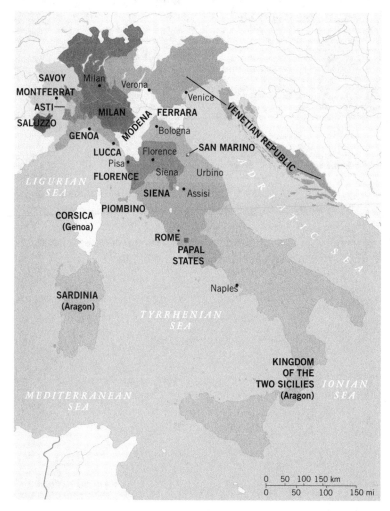

---

*Otto of Freising, in case you need to know his name. (You won't.)

1450: Italy vs. Western Europe	
Italy	**Western Europe**
Urban	Rural
Merchant class dominant	Landed class dominant
Modern commercial infrastructure	Medieval commercial infrastructure
Free republicanism	Monarchies
Little feudalism	Lots of feudalism

Humanism

The Italian Renaissance kickstarted a new way of looking at humans—as individuals! Without God! This was a new idea, because...

Renaissance Italians instead learned to view humans as individuals—and it was the ancient Greeks who taught them this.

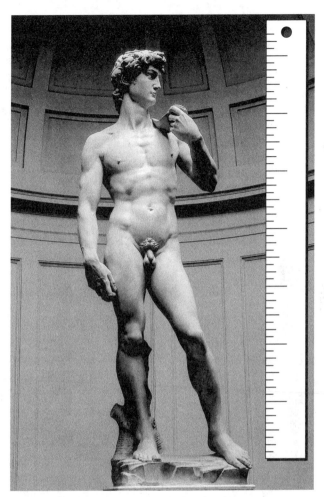

"Man is the measure of all things." —*Protagoras*

 ## *Did You Know?*

The Greek influence upon the sculpture *David* can be seen even in his posture, which the Italians call *contrapposto!*

The rediscovery of Plato led to the rediscovery of one strand of philosophy called **Neoplatonism**. There was even a school, the **Florentine Platonic Academy**, dedicated to metaphysical and numerical exploration of the universe, a study known as **hermeticism**. This may sound weird now, but it wasn't back then—some of the most important philosophical figures in the Renaissance, such as **Pico della Mirandola** and **Lorenzo Valla**, explored this branch of thought.

 ## Did You Know?

The Matrix trilogy was heavily influenced by Neoplatonism, including the name of the main character—Neo!

🔔 **Civic humanism** is the term given to the moral, social, and political philosophy that grew up in the Florentine region. The best representation of this philosophy was the idea of the **Renaissance man**, a well-rounded individual who is committed to actively participating in the political life of the republic. It found full expression in Castiglione's **The Book of the Courtier,** a handbook of the way in which a man should conduct himself in public life. Likewise, **Lorenzo Valla** proved the Donation of Constantine was a forgery, which helped his patron gain power over the papacy. **Leonardo Bruni**, meanwhile, coined the term *studia humanitatis*, which refers to the new course of humanistic education (separate from the metaphysics and theology of the medieval era).

Renaissance Art ❗

Renaissance artists were often supported by wealthy individuals known as **patrons,** who were often kings, princes, cardinals, merchants, or even groups such as convents or monasteries. The patron usually saw support of the arts as a means of achieving social status within the community.

Furthermore, the individualism that was seen in philosophy and education was also present in art. Renaissance painters began using **single-point perspective**, meaning that they drew from a linear perspective using a horizon line and vanishing point.

Medieval

Renaissance

Unlike medieval artists, Renaissance artists also employed **chiaroscuro**, which is the play of light and shadow against a subject.

High Renaissance

The high point of the Renaissance era stretched from 1490 to 1527. During this time, some of the most iconic works of the age—and arguably in all of European history—were created.

Leonardo da Vinci painted his iconic *Mona Lisa*.

Rafael painted *The School of Athens*, featuring a lineup of famous classical philosophers.

Michelangelo painted the Sistine Chapel and carved *David*.

The **Late Renaissance**, also called the period of **Mannerism**, extended from 1530 to the end of the century. It was marked by unnatural elegance, elongated and stylized poses, excessive sophistication, and artificial qualities. Artists included Gentileschi, Bernini, and El Greco.

 ## *Did You Know?*

The rock group Guns 'n' Roses put a figure from *The School of Athens* on the cover of one of its albums!

Northern Renaissance—
Christian Humanists ❗

As time went on, merchants and scholars slowly carried the intellectual and artistic innovations of humanism out of Italy to northern Europe.

Paying close attention to these ideas was **Desiderius Erasmus**, a Polish scholar and devout Catholic. Using the new practice of textual criticism, Erasmus analyzed the New Testament of the Bible and began replacing medieval scholastic texts with more contemporary humanistic texts. Two of his own books are classics of the era. One, *Handbook of a Christian Knight*, urged readers to study the Scriptures directly without interpretation. The other, *In Praise of Folly*, savagely mocked the abuses of the Catholic Church...even though Erasmus himself was a Catholic priest!

Here's a good memory trick: *Erasmus laid the egg that Luther hatched*! Meaning that Erasmus's ideas were later put into practice by the Protestants.

In England, another Northern humanist, **Sir Thomas More**, published *Utopia,* a story that promoted a radical view of an imaginary world without private property. He was executed by King Henry VIII for refusing to recognize the annulment of the monarch's first marriage and his supremacy.

Northern Renaissance—Art and Literature ⓘ

Say the word *art* to some folks and they immediately think of Renaissance Italy. But the painters of the Renaissance in northern Italy are just as good, and to some opinions, maybe even better. In the German-speaking regions and the Netherlands, these painters became known for their **minute attention to detail**. These painters also portrayed dark **Gothic** elements in their works.

For example, **Hieronymous Bosch** painted surreal scenes of hellish torture on immense **triptychs** (three-sided panels). His work was apocalyptic and weird and yet somehow totally modern.

Panel from the Triptych of *The Temptation of St. Anthony* by Hieronymus Bosch

In England, the Renaissance emerged mostly in literature around the turn of the 17th century. The Elizabethan Renaissance (named for Elizabeth I) was a special hotbed of literary talent. **Ben Jonson** popularized the humorous comedy. Playwright **Christopher Marlowe** was considered the hottest tragedian in 1500 years until he was killed under mysterious circumstances.

The undisputed king of English letters was (and is) **William Shakespeare**. After his numerous sonnets—all written before the age of 30—he turned to writing stage plays. He did everything—comedies, tragedies, romances, histories, and even a few weird ones. He's remembered for his verbal dexterity, his invention of new words, and his deep multilayered characters.

 ## *Did You Know?*

Of Shakespeare's 32 plays, the only one featuring an original plot was *The Tempest*. All the others were stolen from Italian playwrights or history books.

The Protestant Reformation

It was the biggest religious revolution in European history. The Catholic Church had dominated European culture, religion, trade, art, and architecture for well over a thousand years. However, a few radical freethinkers on the northern edge of the continent protested and squirmed free of its grasp.

The ABCs of Reasons for the Protestant Reformation

1. **A**nticlericalism—There existed a deep opposition to Catholic priests for their political and social power.
2. **B**lack Plague—A third of the European population had died, which destabilized the Church's power.
3. **C**haucer's *The Canterbury Tales*—The crimes perpetuated by the friar, the pardoner, and other Catholic figures prepared the ground for larger protest.

4. **D**ivided Catholic Church—The papacy's move to Avignon had created two popes, a period known as the Great Schism.
5. **E**mbezzling peasants' money through the sale of indulgences—**Johann Tetzel**, a Dominican friar, made a fortune selling get-out-of-hell cards to medieval peasants.
6. **F**oundation of pietism—Studying the Bible directly, and living a morally upright life, was offered as a way to bypass Catholic corruption.
7. **G**utenberg's invention of the printing press—The rapid and cheaper method of printing books allowed literate Protestants to read and study the Bible at home for the first time.

This alphabet soup had been simmering for decades. The pot eventually had to boil over, and the man who turned up the heat would become the most important religious figure in European history.

Martin Luther

Whether he actually posted **Ninety-Five Theses** to the front door of his church in Wittgenstein—there are some who believe he quietly mailed them to his archbishop—doesn't matter. In his rejection of Catholic doctrine, Luther became the face of the biggest European religious movement of the last thousand years.

Topic	Catholic Church	Protestant Lutherans
Highest authority?	The pope	The Bible
Highest *local* authority?	The priesthood	The "priesthood of all believers"
Salvation?	Earned by good deeds	Earned by "faith alone"
Bible study?	Listen to priest read at mass	Read alone at home
Number of sacraments?	Seven	Two
Preferred Bible language?	Latin	Local vernacular

The Catholic Church didn't take kindly to his radical changes. **Pope Leo X** asked Luther to recant some of his beliefs—and when Luther refused, the pope excommunicated him. He gathered other enemies too, most notably **Johann Eck**, who branded him a heretic for his belief that Catholic Church teachings weren't infallible. Luther appeared before the **Diet of Worms***, an assembly of the estates of the Holy Roman Empire, and again refused to recant. He was arrested and held in Wartburg for a year. Soon after, he began to assemble his own new church, dubbed **Lutheranism**. This new form of Christianity featured a decentralized structure, a reduced number of sacraments, and a rejection of transubstantiation. The **Augsburg Confession** became its most important document of faith.

Indie bands or Protestant reformers?

John Wycliffe and the Lollards
Kill-Sin Pimple
Albert of Hohenzollern and the Fuggers
Childish Gambino

All early Protestants. (Except the last one. His name is actually Donald.)

---

*The Princeton Review does not recommend a diet of worms.

Spread of Protestantism

The German-speaking people saw Luther hoist the flag of protest…and promptly joined in. However, as in any movement, the various sects began to fracture the movement. The **German Peasants' Revolt of 1525** highlighted these divisions, as the peasants' disorganized popular revolt was supported by the new Anabaptists. However, it was brutally put down by the highly organized and well-funded aristocracy—and Luther supported the aristocracy, angrily denouncing the violent mob as doing the work of the devil. He even wrote a book called *Against the Murderous, Thieving Hordes of Peasants*.

Three decades later, the divisions grew so stark that the Holy Roman Emperor, Charles V, decided to put everything to bed. He hammered out a treaty with all the small German princes allowing them sovereignty. In other words, each German principality got to choose whether it would remain Catholic or go Lutheran. The result was the first official division of a European state into Catholic and Protestant factions. Though the Lutherans' time had arrived, the agreement refused to recognize the more radical sects of Protestantism.

Protestants Gone Wild

The more radical sects of the Protestant movement were the **Anabaptists** and the **Antitrinitarians**.

The only radical thing that the Anabaptists did was reject the practice of infant baptism, preferring to baptize believers when they were adults. Overall, they were a peaceful separatist group—with one very notable exception. The Anabaptists are unfortunately remembered today for their violent, unsuccessful attempt to establish a communal sectarian government in the town of **Münster**. After a year of their rule, the town was besieged and overthrown, and the revolutionary Anabaptist leaders were executed and their bodies hung in cages in the town square.

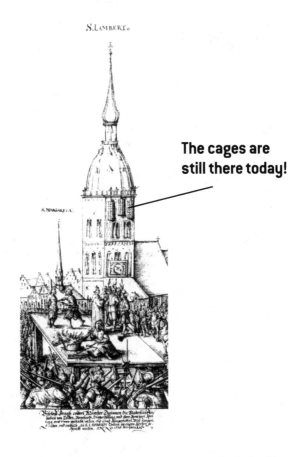

The cages are still there today!

As their name implies, the Antitrinitarians rejected the Catholic idea that God was split into three parts—the Father, the Son, and the Holy Spirit. Instead, they promoted the idea that God was a single entity. This idea spread quickly, especially in England and Scotland, but its adherents never organized themselves into a church the way, for example, the Lutherans did.

 Did You Know?

In the United States, the Amish and Mennonite people are descendants of the original Anabaptists!

Calvin and Zwingli

From today's perspective, **John Calvin** has enjoyed the longest-lasting influence, even more than Luther. A Frenchman who fled to Switzerland, Calvin attacked the use of religious images in places of worship and promoted **predestination**—the idea that God has already selected who will be sent to heaven and who will burn in hell. He believed in a theocratic state of Christian governance and even became the supreme leader of the city of Geneva, where he banned all forms of art and ordered the execution of nearly 60 people. His ideas, expressed in his book *Institutes of the Christian Religion,* formed the backbone of several of today's most popular Protestant groups, including Presbyterians, Congregational, Reformed, Unitarianism, and many groups of Baptists.

Did You Know?

The first Puritan settlers in the United States were Calvinists!

Like Calvin, **Huldrych Zwingli** attacked ecclesiastical corruption and the use of images. Like Calvin, he rejected the idea of transubstantiation and established a small theocracy in the city of Zurich. *Unlike* Calvin, however, Zwingli was theologically even more radical, demanding that people stop fasting during Lent. He was killed while waging an unsuccessful blockade of food shipments to Catholic regions.

"The King's Great Matter"

The biggest figure in the English Reformation was **Henry VIII**. His first marriage, to **Catherine of Aragon**, is legendary—because she hadn't given him any sons, he decided to look elsewhere. Then, as older men sometimes do, he fell in love with a young lady-in-waiting, **Anne Boleyn**. Henry wanted an annulment, but the Pope wouldn't allow it, so the king simply announced supremacy over the Catholic Church. It was a bold move, but Parliament followed, and over the next seven years the **English Reformation Parliament** passed a series of laws designed to punish the Catholic Church—and creating the Church of England (known later as the Anglican Church). A schism opened between London and Rome.

Although Henry received the annulment of his marriage to Catherine, his second marriage to Anne Boleyn turned out even worse. Because she, too, failed to produce any sons, Henry invented a story about her supposed adultery and plot to murder him. It was enough to get her beheaded. His third wife, **Jane Seymour**, died in childbirth—ironically, to a son, the future Edward VI.

Meanwhile, the king's religious power was solidified with two sets of parliamentary acts. The **Acts of Supremacy** designated the English monarch the head of the Church of England. The **Act of Appeals**, meanwhile, forbade all appeals to the pope.

Henry VIII's daughter, **Mary Tudor**, better known as "Bloody Mary," reigned for five years. During this time, she tried to reinstate Catholicism—and burned nearly 300 Protestant dissenters at the stake in the process! (Does the nickname make sense now?) Her successor, **Elizabeth I** (the daughter of Anne Boleyn) reversed those policies, making Protestantism the main form of Christianity in England.

The Counter Reformation: The Pope Strikes Back 🔋

Isaac Newton said, "For every action, there is an equal and opposite reaction." This applies to religious movements too—and you can imagine that the Catholic Church reacted badly to the Protestant eruption. The pope's influence in the north was very limited, but in the Mediterranean area things went differently.

1. The Inquisition 🔋

Despite its name, the Inquisition wasn't a single program—it was actually three. The **Roman Inquisition** was a system of Catholic tribunals in the late 16th century that investigated people who had committed crimes against Catholic religious doctrines. They also maintained a list of banned books known as the **Index**. Another inquisition, the **Spanish Inquisition**, occurred almost a century earlier, and was designed to identify heretics from those who had supposedly converted from Judaism and Islam. (The third was the **Portuguese Inquisition**.) Yes, these programs used torture—but also many other methods of censure, such as excommunication.

The Jesuits

The Inquisition

The Council of Trent

2. The Jesuits ❗

A wounded Spanish noble, **Ignatius Loyola**, was recuperating in a hospital when he came to the realization that God was calling him to become a priest. So he founded a new order of priests, the **Society of Jesus**, which became known for its strict behavior and education. The pope approved and soon began sending them on missions around the world as ambassadors. They became known as "God's soldiers" and were considered exemplars of what Catholic priests could be.

3. The Council of Trent ❗

To review its own shortcomings, the Catholic Church called the **Council of Trent** in 1545. Lasting 20 years, this ecumenical council slowly looked over church doctrines ranging from original sin to sacraments to the Mass. In the end, it made clarifications to Catholic theology—such as demanding that all clergy be educated—but no doctrines were actually altered. Then, as now, Catholic teachings were viewed as infallible. This is the heart of the Counter Reformation.

 Did You Know?

Pope Francis, elected in 2013, is the first Jesuit pope…as well as the first pope from South America!

Europe 1470: BEFORE THE PROTESTANT REVOLUTION.

Europe 1570: AFTER THE PROTESTANT REVOLUTION.

FINLAND

NORWAY

SWEDEN

ESTONIA

SCOTLAND

LATVIA

DENMARK

LITHUANIA

RUSSIA

IRELAND

ENGLAND

THE NETHERLANDS

POLAND

GERMANY

BELGIUM

CZECHOSLOVAKIA

SLOVAKIA

FRANCE

SWITZERLAND

AUSTRIA

HUNGARY

SLOVENIA

CROATIA

ITALY

PORTUGAL

SPAIN

| | Roman Catholic |
| | Protestant |

Iberia Takes Over the World ❗

The Spanish and the Portuguese were Europe's primary explorers in the 16th century (with England placing a distant third). They both established global empires.

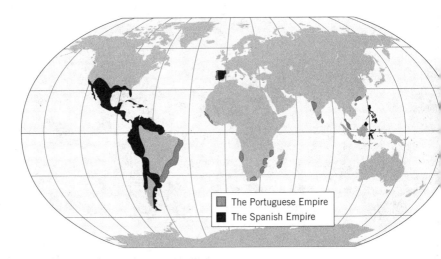

But there were big differences between the two.

	Spanish	Portuguese
Type of empire?	Land	Sea
Source of wealth?	Mining precious metals	Sugar, spices, and slaves
Used indigenous labor?	Yes	No
Region of the world?	The Americas	The Americas, Africa, Asia
Colonial presence?	Coastal and interior regions	Coastal regions only

As usual, advances in technology made all this wandering possible. New navigation devices such as the **compass**, **astrolabe**, and **quadrant** guided ships to far-flung lands. **Guns** and **gunpowder** helped them to easily conquer indigenous peoples. And though **horses** were neither new nor technological, the Spanish brought them to the Americas for the first time.

Celebrity Conquistadores

They were the rock stars of the Age of Exploration—the ship captains who fearlessly sailed to distant lands and brought back riches. Which ones should you know?

The Portuguese

1. **Prince Henry the Navigator** was the grandfather of the era. He went to Madeira, the Azores, and the west coast of Africa. ●●●

2. **Bartolomeu Dias** was the first European to sail to the southern tip of Africa, the Cape of Good Hope. Dias wanted to go further, but his crew mutinied and forced him to turn back. ❶

3. **Vasco da Gama** was the first European to reach India by sea. This opened the door to global imperialism. ❶

The Spanish

1. **Christopher Columbus** was an Italian explorer who sailed for the Spanish throne. His voyage to the West in search of a passage to India resulted in the discovery of the Americas, the creation of trade routes, and the establishment of the transatlantic slave trade. ❶

2. **Ferdinand Magellan** was a Portuguese captain who, like Columbus, sailed for the Spanish throne. He organized the first expedition to circumnavigate (sail around) the entire world! Though he was killed by indigenous people in the Philippines, his ship and crew completed the journey. ❶

3. **Hernán Cortés** began the Spanish colonization of the Americas. He conquered the Aztec empire and claimed Mexico for the Spanish crown, calling the area New Spain—though it encompassed areas including North, Central, and South America. ❶

4. **Francisco Pizarro**, an illiterate Spanish pig farmer, led the expedition that eventually conquered the Inca Empire in modern-day Peru, Bolivia, and Chile. His life story is brutal but remarkable. ❶

Did You Know?

Within 25 years of Columbus's arrival on Hispaniola, most of the indigenous population had died of enslavement, massacre, or disease!

The Development of Monarchical States

Several factors contributed to the rise of monarchical states in Europe in the 15th and 16th centuries:

1. **The end of The Hundred Years' War** left a lot of unemployed soldiers, whom the wealthy families and the monarch hired to assert their power.
2. The monarchs took the right (granted by representative assemblies) to consistently **tax the citizenry**. Before this era, taxing was occasional and disorganized.
3. The **weakness of the papacy** allowed the monarchs to gain control of their national churches and use local clergy to mold public opinion toward the others.

These monarchs did grow in power during this time, but the nobility and clergy always were ready to oppose them if they appeared to be taking more power than seemed fair. And those groups held most of the national wealth as well.

Italy: Settling Down ❗

By 1454, the northern city-states of the Italian peninsula had been squabbling for centuries.* These disagreements of the period had multiple causes and were sometimes egged on by people desperate to make their own fortune. Case in point: **Niccolo Machiavelli** wrote *The Prince*—a handbook demonstrating the most ruthless ways to keep power—as a way of getting back into the good graces of Lorenzo de' Medici, the Florentine *doge* who had cast him aside as an advisor.

However, the **Treaty of Lodi** finally brought three of the city-states—Florence, Milan, and Naples—into a balance of power that stabilized the northern region. It lasted only 50 years, but the peace showed that if an agreement could be made on the Italian peninsula, it could be made anywhere.

England: Heating Up ❗

From 1455 to 1487, a series of small civil wars known as the **Wars of the Roses** rocked England. Two rival families, the House of York and the House of Lancaster, vied for control of the throne. The wars ended with Richard III—yes, the hunchback—being defeated by **Henry Tudor**, a distant relative of the Lancaster family. With all the male heirs in both houses having been killed, he took the throne, married a York, and the war was finished.

His dynasty, the **Tudors**, ruled for almost 120 years. They were the type of family that makes for great television—fighting, killing, making up, killing again. Here's the progression through five monarchs:

1. Henry VII (Henry Tudor)
2. Henry VIII
3. Edward VI
4. Mary I
5. Elizabeth I

---

*Let's face it; they're still squabbling, sort of. Mostly about food.

Of these five individuals, Elizabeth I was the most consequential, ruling for almost 45 years and famously defeating the **Spanish Armada**. A lover of the arts, she used white makeup to look extra pale, played the lute, and participated in new dance crazes such as *la volta*. In general, Elizabeth presided over a period of cultural flourishing known as the **English Renaissance**. However, the so-called "**Virgin Queen**" also had issues with **Mary, Queen of Scots,** who she was convinced wanted to occupy the English throne. She imprisoned Mary for 19 years before reluctantly beheading her. Elizabeth, however, was the last Tudor. When she died without an heir in 1603, it was her dead rival Mary's son, James VI of Scotland, who took over the English throne, renaming himself **James I**. The irony!

Spain: "Winning" the Gold ❗

King Ferdinand and Queen Isabella remade the face of Iberia at the end of the 15th century. What's often forgotten, however, is that their marriage itself united two separate northern kingdoms, Castile and Aragon.

With that accomplished, Ferdinand and Isabella consolidated all the military forces of the Christian north to oppose the Moors (African Muslims) that had occupied the south of Spain for 700 years. Sweeping down from the north, they waged the **Reconquista,** pushing the Moors out of Spain in a few short years. Then Ferdinand and Isabella set about expelling the Jews in what has become known as the **Spanish Inquisition**. About half of the Jews left the country, while the other half converted (or claimed to convert) to Christianity.

Some people are born lucky, and some people are **Charles V**. In the 16th century, this 19-year-old Habsburg monarch inherited from his family *three* different areas—the Netherlands, Austria, and Spain.* That wasn't enough, and Charles attempted to build a global Christian empire, which France and the Ottoman Empire resisted.

To this end, Charles also signed the **Peace of Augsburg** with the Schmalkaldic League (yes, that's its real name). This treaty officially allowed the rulers of small German principalities to determine their own religion, whether Catholic or Lutheran. It was a victory for Protestantism.**

---

*What was left of the Holy Roman Empire, which was neither holy, nor Roman, nor an empire.

**But not for Calvinism. They agreed Calvinism should stay illegal, which it was for another century.

Ultimately Charles gave up the dream, abdicated the throne, and sliced the Holy Roman Empire in half. He handed over the Austrian part of this empire to his brother **Ferdinand**, and most of the other regions to his son **Philip II**.

His son was maybe even luckier than his dad. Philip II ruled for 42 years, presiding over the **Golden Age of Spain**. It was literally golden, with tons of gold and silver flowing into its banks from the colonies in the New World. In fact, Philip's only real trouble came from religion. Though he successfully suppressed Protestantism in Spain, he never was able to do the same in his northern Habsburg holdings. When Elizabeth I allied her English troops with Protestant rebels in the Netherlands—which was his territory—Philip launched the first of many **Spanish Armadas** to attack England. All of them failed.

Artistically, the Golden Age of Spain was marked by writers such as Cervantes, who penned the classic story of **Don Quixote** and his sidekick Sancho Panza. In the visual arts, **El Greco** created fantastic canvases of expressionistic imagination.

France: Losing Its Religion

Like other monarchical nations of this era, Catholic France grappled with the question of how to handle Protestantism. Unlike the other wars of religion, however, millions of people were killed in the **French Wars of Religion** in the late 16th century. This saw Catholics pitted against Huguenots (who were French Protestants, mostly Calvinists).

The players: the queen, **Catherine de' Medici**. Fighting to succeed her were members of the **House of Guise** (solidly Catholic), who vied with the **House of Condé** (sympathetic with the Huguenots). In the end, Catherine sided with Guise and even instigated the **St. Bartholomew's Day Massacre**, in which roving bands of Catholics slaughtered Huguenots in the streets of Paris. In the following weeks and months, this spread across the kingdom, resulting in the worst Protestant massacre in the history of Europe—and a total breakdown of state control.

A quarter century later, the issue was finally put to bed when Henry of Navarre, a Huguenot, converted to Catholicism and took the throne as **Henry IV**. A beloved king in French history—and the first of the Bourbon dynasty—he immediately issued the **Edict of Nantes**, which gave substantial rights and freedoms to the Huguenots. The edict held for almost a century, when Louis XIV revoked it.

 ### Did You Know?

Henry IV came to power by winning the *War of the Three Henrys*—against Henry III and Henry of Lorraine!

Thirty Years' War

Lasting from 1618 to 1648, it was the longest-lasting, most expensive, most destructive, and possibly most pointless war in European history. Eight million people died of violence, plague, and famine.

The cause? The new Holy Roman Emperor* **Ferdinand II** had forced northern Protestants to start practicing Catholicism, in violation of the Peace of Augsburg.

The fighting started locally, in what is today Germany, but it didn't stay local. The arguments spread throughout Europe, growing in size, as various monarchs saw their opportunity to swing the continent either more Catholic or more Protestant. These monarchs hired **mercenary armies**— soldiers who fought for money—to do the violence.

One early event that put the conflict into hyperdrive occurred in **Bohemia** in 1619, when Protestants ousted the Habsburgs and elected their own Calvinist leader, **Frederick V**, as King of Bohemia. Ferdinand II's mercenary forces brutally defeated their army. As a result, Bohemia and the Czech region never again returned to Protestantism. The whole area remains Catholic even to this day.

---

*Which was still not holy, not Roman, and not an empire.

By the time this ultimate war of religion sputtered to an end—with the signing of the **Peace of Westphalia**—the Thirty Years' War had bankrupted many European nations. The populations of German regions, Bohemia, Italy, and others had been devastated. In fact, the only two countries that emerged unscathed from the war were France and especially the **Dutch Republic,** which soon entered into its own Golden Age, becoming one of the world's premier economic and naval powers.

Involvement in Thirty Years' War

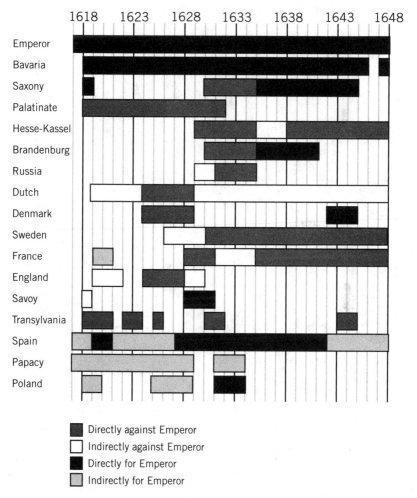

Year(s)	Event
1341	Petrarch crowned Poet Laureate in Rome
1378	Ciompi Revolt
1378	Black Death hits Europe
1387	Chaucer starts *The Canterbury Tales*
1397	Establishment of the Medici Bank
1403	Alberti begins work on the doors of the baptistery in Florence
1405	Christine de Pisan's *City of Ladies*
1406	Florence conquers Pisa
1415	Burning at the stake of Jan Hus at the Council of Constance
1415	Prince Henry the Navigator participates in capture of Ceuta in northwestern Africa
1417	Great Schism comes to an end
1420s	Development of single-point perspective
1440	Lorenzo Valla's *On the Donation of Constantine*
1440s	Donatello's *David*
1452	Gutenberg prints Bible
1453	End of the Hundred Years' War
1453	Fall of Constantinople
1454	Treaty of Lodi

Year(s)	Event
1469	Marriage of Ferdinand of Aragon to Isabella of Castile
1485	Henry VII begins Tudor dynasty following the Battle of Bosworth Field
1486	Pico's *Oration on the Dignity of Man*
1487	Bartholomew Dias sails around Cape of Good Hope
1490	Ludovico il Moro becomes despot of Milan
1492	Columbus leaves Spain for what he believes will be Asia
1492	Expulsion of the Jews from Spain
1492	*Reconquista* of Spain completed
1492	Lorenzo de Medici dies
1494	King Charles VIII of France invades Italy
1494	The Treaty of Tordesillas divides the discoveries in the New World between Spain and Portugal
1498	Vasco da Gama reaches the coast of India
1498	Burning of Savonarola
1501	Michelangelo's *David*
1503	Leonardo's *Mona Lisa*
1509	Raphael's *School of Athens*
1513	Machiavelli writes *The Prince*
1515	Erasmus's *In Praise of Folly*

Year(s)	Event
1516	More's *Utopia*
1517	Luther's *95 Theses*
1519	Charles V becomes Holy Roman Emperor
1519	Ferdinand Magellan sets out to circumnavigate the globe
1519	Hernán Cortés lands on the coast of Mexico
1521	Luther called before the Diet of Worms
1522	Ignatius Loyola begins *The Spiritual Exercises*
1525	German Peasant Revolt
1528	Castiglione's *The Book of the Courtier*
1529	Diet of Speyer
1529	Henry VIII summons the "Reformation Parliament"
1531	Zwingli dies in battle
1531	Francisco Pizarro sets out for Peru
1534	Henry VIII's Act of Supremacy
1534	Anabaptists seize Munster
1535	Sir Thomas More executed by Henry VIII
1536	Calvin publishes first edition of his *Institutes of the Christian Religion*
1540	Jesuits receive official papal sanction as religious order

Year(s)	Event
1540	Henry VIII marries Anne Boleyn
1540s	Schmalkaldic War
1543	Copernicus publishes *On the Revolutions of the Celestial Spheres*
1543	Andreas Vesalius writes *De humani corporis fabrica* with its critique of the anatomical work of Galen
1545	Council of Trent convenes
1553	End of reign of Edward VI of England
1553	Michael Servetus burned at the stake in Geneva
1555	Peace of Augsburg
1556	Philip II becomes King of Spain after Charles V abdicates
1558	Death of Queen Mary of England
1558	Beginning of reign of Elizabeth Tudor
1559	Frederick III of the Palatinate converts to Calvinism
1559	Death of King Henry II of France
1559	Elizabethan religious settlement
1562	Beginning of the French Wars of Religion
1571	Battle of Lepanto

Year(s)	Event
1572	St. Bartholomew's Day Massacre during the French Wars of Religion
1587	Execution of Mary, Queen of Scots
1588	Failure of the Spanish Armada to invade England
1589	Henry Bourbon becomes King Henry IV
1593	Henry IV converts to Catholicism
1598	Edict of Nantes
1600	Giordano Bruno burned at the stake
1602	First known performance of Shakespeare's *Hamlet*
1602	Dutch East India Company established
1603	James I becomes king following death of Elizabeth
1603	Michael Romanov begins new dynasty in Russia
1605	Cervantes publishes first part of *Don Quixote*
1607	Founding colony at Jamestown
1610	Assassination of Henry IV
1610	Galileo begins astronomical observations with his telescope
1613	Galileo publishes *Letters on Sunspots*
1616	William Harvey announces his discovery of the circulatory system
1618	Johannes Kepler reveals his third and final law of planetary motion

Year(s)	Event
1618	Beginning of the Thirty Years' War
1620	Battle of White Mountain
1620	Founding of Plymouth Colony
1620	Francis Bacon publishes *Novum Organum*
1624	Cardinal Richelieu becomes Louis XIII's chief minister
1625	Charles I becomes king upon death of James I
1628	Petition of Right
1628	Murder of the Duke at Buckingham
1629	Edict of Restitution
1629	Personal Rule of Charles I begins and will last 11 years
1632	Gustavus Adolphus dies at the Battle of Lutzen
1632	Galileo's *Dialogue on the Two Chief Systems of the World*
1633	Trial of Galileo
1633	Murder of Albrecht von Wallenstein
1637	Charles introduces the Book of Common Prayer into Scotland
1637	René Descartes publishes *Discourse on the Mind*
1640	Beginning of the reign of Frederick William (Great Elector)
1640	Charles forced to summon Parliament to deal with Scottish revolt

Year(s)	Event
1641	Rebellion in Ireland
1642	Execution of the Earl of Strafford
1642	Issuing of Grand Remonstrance
1642	Beginning of English Revolution
1643	Five-year-old Louis XIV becomes King of France
1645	Execution of Archbishop Laud
1648	Peace of Westphalia

CHAPTER 2

Monarchical States to Napoleon: c. 1648–c. 1815

England—Power to the People

Here's the big idea. After a century of internal conflict and civil war, England finally got rid of the **divine right of kings** and replaced it with a **constitutional monarchy** (1689). In other words, the king's power to rule no longer came from God. The king's power to rule came from the people.

The royal history of England in the 17th century (dominated by the **Stuart** dynasty) is easy to remember as a palindrome: **JCOCJ.*** The first two letters and the last two letters represent members of the Stuart family. The one in the middle, Oliver Cromwell, refused to be called King.

James I   Charles I   Oliver Cromwell   Charles II   James II

James VI of Scotland became **James I** of England in 1603 and was the first monarch to hold both thrones simultaneously. Though he was a Protestant—he sponsored the translation of the Bible famously known as the **King James Bible**—he was suspected of being a closet Catholic because of his **"no bishop, no king"** policy. This was a reference to the power of the Anglican bishops being attached to the power of the king, which was then interpreted as an attack upon the **Puritans**, a renegade group of extreme Protestants.

He also promoted a three-part program of success:

1. Unite England with Scotland
2. Create a continental standing army
3. Set up a new royal finance system

The program wasn't successful. In politics, James I is popularly remembered for his **clashes with Parliament**, particularly over money and funding. He ended up dissolving several Parliaments and ruling alone.

---

*Other palindromes include: ABBA; a man, a plan, a canal, Panama; and everyone's favorite, tacocat.

Did You Know?

An assassination attempt on James I was foiled when one of the conspirators, Guy Fawkes, was discovered hiding with a barrel of gunpowder in the basement of Parliament. His failure has become a national holiday: November 5, Guy Fawkes Day.

Under **Charles I** (son of James I), the relationship between king and Parliament grew even worse. In the **tonnage and poundage** conflict, for example, Parliament granted Charles the right to tax custom duties for only one year. He'd expected them for life—and continued the tax without Parliament's consent. Later, when Parliament refused to fund his foreign wars, Charles levied other taxes and even forced them to put up soldiers from the royal army. In response, Parliament passed the **Petition of Rights**, a major defense of individual liberties.

In Parliament, **John Eliot** led a series of protests known as the **Three Revolutions**, which was an objection to the growing Arminian faction of the Church of England, a branch that was viewed as suspiciously crypto-Catholic. He even encouraged merchants to stop paying the tonnage and poundage taxes. Furious, Charles I dissolved Parliament and arrested all the Parliamentary leaders. It didn't meet again for 11 years.

This era was called the **Personal Rule** of Charles I, though his enemies called it flat-out tyranny. He raised money by reviving ancient, forgotten forms of taxes such as **ship-money**, a medieval custom that required coastal towns to pay for naval defenses. A man named **John Hampden** refused to pay and went to court, winning a moral victory against the king's heavy hand.

Charles I also desired to bring Scotland closer to England*, causing Archbishop Laud to introduce a common liturgy to both kingdoms. This was the **Book of Common Prayer**, and Scottish Presbyterians erupted in violence at the imposition. This hostility resulted in the signing of the **Scottish National Covenant** and the **Bishops' Wars**, during which time

---

*Not *geographically* closer, although that would be quite a feat! *Politically* and *religiously* closer.

Scotland invaded England. Because the English treasury was nearly empty, and because Charles I had run out of creative ways to drum up money, he was forced to call Parliament again. This one, called the **Short Parliament**, ended his Personal Rule.

Finally, in 1641, during the **Long Parliament**, various members of Parliament presented Charles I with a list of complaints about his behavior. This was called the **Grand Remonstrance**, calling for the removal of all bishops from Parliament. Charles I thought about it and then finally denied the request. This marked the beginning of the **English Civil War** (1642 to 1651).

An important lesson there for would-be tyrants, don't you think? Following that came an 11-year interregnum during which there was no king, only a Lord Protector—**Oliver Cromwell**. A Puritan, he wore black clothing and carried a briefcase. This period of bourgeoisie republic is called the **Commonwealth**, and it was marked by political movements such as the **Levellers** (populists) and the **Diggers** (agricultural radicals).

However, it was a period of artistic repression too—hey, the Puritans were in charge—and many theaters were forced to close during this time. When Cromwell finally died, **Charles II**—son of executed Charles I— was welcomed to the throne. This return of the Stuarts is known as the **Restoration**, not only because of the return of the house of Stuart, but also because the arts exploded into life after 11 years of forced hibernation. His reign, though long, was not marked by much except continued religious squabbling.

His brother, **James II**, proved to be the undoing of the Stuarts. His short three-year reign was cut short when he was suspected of plotting a return to absolute power, like his father and grandfather. Another problem was his belief in religious liberty, which the Anglican establishment interpreted as suspected Catholicism. This suspicion grew when James II refused to submit to the **Test Acts**, which required all officeholders to swear an oath denouncing the Catholic theology. This suspicion continued to grow when he issued the **Declaration of Indulgence**, which exempted Catholics and Protestant dissenters from punishment.

In one of the more interesting twists in history, a group of concerned nobles finally asked James II's son-in-law, **William of Orange**, a Protestant from the Netherlands, to launch an invasion of their own country so they could depose James II. William happily did so, James II fled the country, and William and his wife Mary took the English throne. This was the **Glorious Revolution**.

The results are now famous—the power couple signed the **Bill of Rights**, which guaranteed parliamentary sovereignty and provided new legal protections for individual citizens. Other acts included*:

Act of Toleration	Provided religious liberty for dissenting Protestants
Act of Settlement	Guaranteed royal succession to Protestants only
Acts of Union	United England and Scotland to form Great Britain
Mutiny Act	Authorized civil law to govern the army, not royal decree

But let's repeat the big idea, because it's that important: after a century of internal conflict and civil war, England finally got rid of the **divine right of kings**...and replaced it with a **constitutional monarchy**.

 Did You Know?

The College of William and Mary in Virginia was named for this royal couple!

---

* Please note that some of these Acts were passed a little bit after 1702, during the reign of Queen Anne.

France—We'll Never Be Royals

In the 17th century, France went the opposite way of its island neighbor. Instead of placing restrictions upon royal power, France expanded and concentrated royal power. It did so under the very long reign of two Bourbon kings—the absolute ruler **Louis XIII** and the even more absolute ruler **Louis XIV**.

Louis XIII took the throne at nine years of age. His mother ruled for him until he was 17, when he exiled her (no joke) and executed many of her followers. Then he consolidated royal power by destroying the estates of defiant nobles and restricting their use of private armies. He also brought France into the **Thirty Years' War** on the side of the Protestants, which was better to counter the Catholic Spain of the Habsburgs, France's traditional enemy. Helping him in all of this was the clever minister, **Cardinal Richelieu**.

Louis XIV, the son of Louis XIII, took the throne at five years of age. Though **Cardinal Mazarin** ruled for him for the next 13 years, upon the cardinal's death, Louis XIV ruled totally alone, as the most absolute of absolute monarchs, for the next 58 years. When young, he was scarred by the **Fronde**, which amplified his desire to wield total, autocratic control. He subscribed to the principle of the **divine right of kings**, as espoused by **Bishop Bossuet**, meaning that God gave him alone the right to rule. To accomplish this, he lured the French nobility to a pleasure palace that he'd constructed near Paris, the **Palace of Versailles**, and then stole power from their home districts while they were distracted with banquets and sex. He consolidated religious power by persecuting Huguenots (French Protestants) by **revoking the Edict of Nantes** and forcing hundreds of thousands to convert to Catholicism.

The Sun King, as Louis XIV became known, pursued a series of costly wars whose primary purpose was revenge and vanity. First came the **Franco-Dutch War**, which saw France, England, and Germany joining forces against the Habsburgs (the Dutch, Spain, and Austria). Next was the **Nine Years' War**, which featured France against seven other nations—and ended with the British nearly doubling the size of their navy. The last one, the **War of Spanish Succession**, was Louis XIV's naked attempt to wrestle control of the Spanish throne by making sure his grandson Philip was allowed to inherit it, as the childless Charles II of Spain had instructed. The other Habsburgs had a different view, to say the least, and after 13 years of fighting, balance was restored to Europe with the **Treaty of Utrecht**.

All of these foreign conflicts depleted the French royal treasury. To raise money, Louis XIV improved the taxation system—and exempted the nobility from paying taxes. He also turned to **Jean-Baptiste Colbert**, his economics minister, to kickstart domestic manufacturing, particularly in ceramics. This was to establish a favorable balance of trade—meaning more exports than imports. This is the definition of **mercantilism**.

"I am the State."

—Louis XIV.

No constitution, no parliament, nothing. There was only him.

 Did You Know?

The Nine Years' War is sometimes called "the first global war"—because it was fought on three continents!

The Netherlands— Let's Go Dutch ❗

The Netherlands enjoyed a period of incredible prosperity in the 17th century, often called the **Golden Age** or "the Dutch Miracle." During this time, Dutch art, science, commerce, and military were the most acclaimed in the world. This success had many causes: the immigration of skilled laborers, the powerful Protestant work ethic (mostly Calvinist), cheap energy sources such as windmills, and pioneering forms of corporate finance.

Because they were masterful shipbuilders (the best in Europe), the Dutch soon came to dominate the seas. An accident of geography made the Netherlands' location the perfect midpoint between the Baltic Sea and the Iberian Peninsula, so they became powerful traders. Gradually, the Dutch branched out, setting their sights on global commerce, and soon controlled all trade with Asia. In fact, the **Dutch East India Company** kept a monopoly on trade with Asia for nearly two hundred years. The Company (as it was called) was the world's first **multinational corporation**, and it was listed on the world's first modern **stock exchange**—two more Dutch innovations.

Another factor in the Netherlands' success was political decentralization. After northern states in the Netherlands separated from the Spanish Habsburg rule, they began to self-rule through a series of meetings of the **States-General**, a body of councilors from different states. It was very informal at first, and no one member held power over any other member. Eventually, this loose arrangement became the de facto government.

There are many ways to measure this Dutch Golden Age. One is by the **increased standard of living**—even middle-class citizens could afford to eat new foods from the New World (such as chocolate) and drink new beverages (such as coffee). Another is by **religious tolerance**. While Catholics were not always met with open arms, in general people in the Netherlands were very hospitable, particularly to Sephardic Jews fleeing Spain and to Huguenots fleeing France. The third measure is by **visual art**. During this century, Dutch painters such as Rembrandt van Rijn, Johannes Vermeer, and Franz Hals became masters of the still-life, landscapes, and portraiture.

The Girl with a Pearl Earring by Johannes Vermeer

 ## *Did You Know?*

The Netherlands enjoyed such a great reputation for shipbuilding that Peter the Great of Russia lived and studied the craft there for nearly a year—in disguise!

Economic and Social Life in Modern Europe ❗

In the 17th century, Europe experienced a period of **economic expansion**. This happened mostly because of increased population, which led to more available manpower, which led to more production, which led to more consumption. Walking hand-in-hand with this change was the **price revolution***. Over a period of about 150 years, ending in the 17th century, Europe experienced enormous inflation. By most estimates, the average cost of goods multiplied by *six times*.**

All this trading and selling created new small fortunes. This meant the birth of a new socioeconomic class, known at the time as the **gentry**, though today we might call it the middle class. This group disrupted the old medieval feudal system with its sudden injection of wealth. In short, the aristocracy didn't understand these commercial wheelers and dealers making money. After all, the aristocrats had inherited all their wealth from their ancestors.

Furthermore, the aristocrats also felt responsible for the poor, uneducated peasants, so they allowed the great unwashed (commoners) to tend to and farm the public lands.*** But the gentry put pressure on the nobles to seal off these public lands, usually by circling them with fences. This is called the **enclosure movement**, and it plunged many of the peasants into desperate poverty. In Protestant England, the Elizabeth-era **Poor Laws** were passed as a way to provide relief to those able-bodied peasants who couldn't find work. In Mediterranean nations, however, the Catholic Church assumed this same responsibility to care for the poor.

---

*DO NOT confuse this with Prince and the Revolution. The only points you'll gain on your test will be cool points.

**This is the sign of a healthy *market economy*. The opposite is a *subsistence economy*, in which prices never change, because nobody is selling anything. Grow food, eat food. Repeat till death.

*** A sentiment known as *noblesse oblige*.

Life in the Fields 🕮

For peasant farmers, life was hard. They were often cold and wet, with homes made of wood or mud. Their total personal belongings could usually fit inside a single chest. They farmed a single strip of the manorial land—and whatever they grew was their food for the entire year. They usually lived and died without ever leaving their village.

Aside from the enclosure movement, the **three-field system** changed agriculture. It involved more plowing of the earth and the addition of legumes (beans), which replenish nitrogen, allowing more land to be planted more often. This system resulted in greater food production and better nutrition, allowing the population to flourish. (The two-field system continued in the Mediterranean area, however.) Nonetheless, the main staples of a peasant diet continued to consist of various grains—mainly beer, bread, and gruel.

Life in the Towns 🕮

Peasants who were squeezed out of common lands often wandered into towns looking for work. To them, this must have been confusing. The houses had a variety of designs and were insulated much better. The townspeople ate a variety of food, including meat. And the workers held a variety of jobs, from butchery to ironmongering.

Most obviously, there were **guilds**, which were structures of skilled workers (apprentice, journeyman, master) that controlled all production. These were holdovers from the medieval era, and the newly rich gentry installed new methods of production, including **piecework** (also called the **putting-out system**), in which workers manufactured fabrics in their own homes. This system devastated the guilds, which meant that a lot of frustrated young men couldn't advance through the ranks. This loss of social mobility led to some of the urban revolts of the era.

Did You Know?

The phrase "town and gown" describes the conflict between townspeople and college students during this era!

The most dominant cities in Europe were shifting too. Italy, Spain, and other Mediterranean countries had dominated trade in the 15th and 16th centuries. However, in the 17th century, England and especially the Netherlands became the economic engines of Europe, with **London**, **Bristol**, **Amsterdam**, and **Antwerp** ballooning in size and influence.

Why did northern Europe begin to enjoy so much economic success at this time? Here are a few factors:

1. One of the main principles of the Protestant Revolution, which was primarily in northern Europe, was the need to prove one's worthiness to God through hard work.
2. Northern Europe produced more technological innovation than Southern Europe.
3. Northern societies were becoming less hierarchical and more individualistic.
4. The three-field system flourished only in northern Europe, allowing better nutrition, larger populations, and more manpower.
5. Northern European countries created innovations in banking, such as joint-stock companies, all of which encouraged risk.

The **British East India Company**, the **Dutch East India Company**, and the **Bank of Amsterdam** are all institutions that represented the economic rise of Northern Europe.

How the Protestant Revolution Changed Social Life

Many European social customs regarding family had been based on nearly a millennium of Catholic tradition. The Protestant Revolution upended many of those customs.

Catholic Custom	Protestant Idea
Marriage is for life.	Divorce is possible.
Beggars and prostitutes are to be pitied and forgiven.	Beggars and prostitutes are morally weak and should be punished.
Unmarried women should be sent to convents.	Unmarried women should live their own lives.
Annual Carnival events are fun!	Annual Carnival events are immoral (because you should be working).
Women cannot lead the church.	Women can become ministers and deacons in some Protestant sects.

The Scientific Revolution

While it's tempting to view historical eras as a series of separate blocks, it's better to view them as a long series of intertwined roots.

Nothing illustrates this better than the 17th-century **Scientific Revolution**. Its causes include almost everything that came in the two hundred years before:

- The **discovery of the New World** brought new plants and animals to Europe.
- The **invention of the printing press** quickly spread news of these discoveries.
- **Rivalries among nation-states** meant increased competition for technological innovation.
- **Renaissance humanism** brought back ancient Greek scientific texts.
- The **Protestant Revolution** showed scientists that it was possible to successfully challenge authority.

❗ Until this time, what passed for science included the medieval writings of **Thomas Aquinas**, who melded the views of Aristotle with the teachings of the Catholic Church to form **scholasticism**.* Additionally, the Church adopted the model of the ancient Roman mathematician and astronomer **Ptolemy**, who had promoted a **geocentric** view of the universe. Another branch of pseudoscience, **alchemy**, researched ways to turn base metals (such as lead) into "noble" metals (such as gold).

❗ The first scientific shot at the Catholic Church was fired by **Nicolaus Copernicus**, an astronomer hired by the Catholic Church in the early 16th century to correct the Julian calendar. While making his measurements, Copernicus came to the uncomfortable conclusion that the sun did not revolve around the earth, as the Ptolemaic system officially held, but that the earth revolved around the sun. This was **heliocentrism**, and Copernicus was hesitant to reveal such a radical theory. Eventually he did publish his findings in his only work, *Concerning the Revolutions of the Heavenly Spheres*, but timidly phrased them as hypotheses—and even dedicated the book to **Pope Paul III**!

💬 Even with such revolutionary ideas, Copernicus didn't make an immediate splash—not until decades later, when **Tycho Brahe** and his student **Johannes Kepler** started to build upon his insights.

❗ The next major scientist, **Galileo Galilei**, also stood on the shoulders of Copernicus. His invention of the telescope—a modified spyglass, which had been invented by the Dutch—helped him make observations about various moons. Unlike Copernicus, Galileo wasn't shy about his findings. He published *Dialogue on the Two Chief Systems of the World* in Italian (not Latin) so that more people could read its radical ideas. Then his supposed friend, **Pope Urban VIII**, put him under house arrest and forced him to recant everything. Galileo reluctantly agreed, but secretly continued publishing his work in more tolerant Protestant countries.

❗ The last and arguably greatest scientist to build on the work of Copernicus was **Isaac Newton**. In his grand work, *Principia*, he solved the question of how planets revolved around the sun in regular ellipses, positing the theory of **gravity** to explain this. In his spare time, he worked in optics, dabbled in alchemy, and invented calculus.

---

*A favorite debate topic of medieval scholastics: *How many angels can dance on the head of a pin?*
(According to the book *Good Omens* by Neil Gaiman and Terry Pratchett, the answer is "one," Aziraphale, since he is the only angel who learned how to dance. So there you go.)

Name these scientists!

From the top: Newton, Galileo, Kepler and Brahe, Copernicus

Other scientists made new inroads into medicine. Before the 17th century, the **humoral theory** of medicine was accepted—a person's sickness was due to an imbalance of the four humours (blood, phlegm, black bile, yellow bile) in the body. New scientific research found otherwise. **William Harvey**, for example, discovered that blood circulates in the body. **Paracelsus** invented the ideas of clinical diagnosis and medical dosages, noting that any substance can be toxic in certain quantities. **Andreas Vesalius** founded modern anatomy through his pioneering practice of dissection.

 Did You Know?

Ancient philosopher Aristotle believed that women had fewer teeth than men had! (No, he never thought of opening a woman's mouth to count. This was before science.)

The Philosophy of Science

By far the most important impact that science had upon intellectual life was the replacement of *deductive reasoning* with *inductive reasoning*.

Deductive reasoning precedes from general principles to specific conclusions. It does not consider any quantifiable information. This was the method of ancient philosophers.

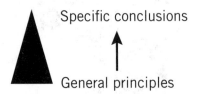
Specific conclusions

General principles

Inductive reasoning precedes from quantifiable information to specific conclusions. It is also called **empiricism**. This was the method of the new scientists.

 Specific conclusions

Evidence from nature
(quantifiable information)

In England, the conflict between the two was known as the **Battle of the Books**. The most vocal proponent of inductive reasoning was **Francis Bacon**, a true Renaissance man who served as lawyer, government official, historian, and essayist. He blasted the medieval scholastics for being hopelessly out of touch with the natural world.

On the other side of the debate, maintaining a steady belief in deductive reasoning, was the French philosopher **René Descartes**. He advocated a **rationalistic philosophy of systematic doubt** that involved reasoning from general principles. At one point, Descartes went so far as to doubt his own existence, which is when he struck upon his most famous quote— "I think; therefore, I am."

The winner: inductive reasoning. The Western world now runs on data.

Another French philosopher, **Blaise Pascal**, has become known for his application of scientific principles to religious thought. One of his most practical thoughts has become known as **Pascal's Wager**, in which he argues from a rational standpoint that we ought to believe in God. Here's his reasoning: *If God exists, we will be rewarded in the afterlife. If God doesn't exist, then it doesn't matter anyways!*

An English political philosopher, **Thomas Hobbes**, was cut from a very different cloth. He'd seen the English Civil Wars up close and was pessimistic about human nature without civilization. As a result, he believed that life outside of society was "solitary, poor, nasty, brutish, and short." As a result, in his book *Leviathan*, Hobbes argued for absolutism—rule by a powerful central government, one that would keep the unruly masses in line. Despite this belief, he admitted that the absolute ruler's power should derive from the people, not from a divine source.

The most influential English political philosopher, however, was **John Locke**. His book *Two Treatises on Government* served as a blueprint for the English Bill of Rights. He believed that all humans are born free, as a *tabula rasa* (blank slate), and that we enter into a **social contract** with our governments, but never give up our inalienable rights to life, liberty, and property.*

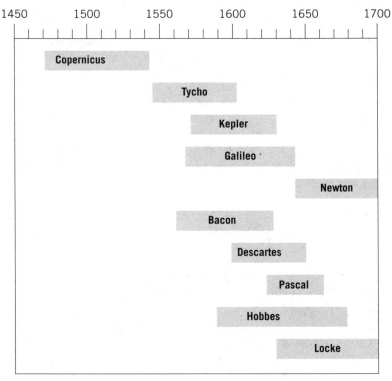

Scientists and Philosophers of the Scientific Revolution, 1450–1700

---

* When Thomas Jefferson stole the phrase for the Declaration of Independence, he changed "property" to "pursuit of happiness."

The Enlightenment ❗

In the 17th century, scientists used reason to understand natural laws. In the 18th century, philosophers used reason to understand human laws. This movement was called the **Enlightenment**. It was defined best by Immanuel Kant, a philosopher who said, "Dare to know."

Like the scientists, the Enlightenment thinkers broke out of the hand-cuffs of tradition. They were intellectually free in ways that Europeans had never been. They met informally in coffee houses, debated in special academies, formed lending libraries (a new concept), and attended *salons* in the homes of wealthy women. They called themselves **philosophes**, and many were centered in France. Many were also **deists**, meaning that they believed in a God who had created the world but then let it operate according to its own laws. In general, deists viewed religion as a private affair and were quite tolerant of all views.

In 1802, William Paley stated his famous watchmaker analogy—that God designed the movements of the universe in the same way that a watchmaker designs a timepiece!

Geographically, the earliest Enlightenment thinkers such as John Locke were based in England, which was admired as a bastion of free thought by philosophers on the continent. Later, the movement grew much stronger as it arrived on the mainland, particularly in France.

Enlightenment Thinkers ❗

Name	Nation	Field	Belief(s)	Book
Adam Smith	Scotland	Economics	Invisible hand of the market	*The Wealth of Nations*
David Hume	Scotland	Religion	Skepticism; empiricism	*A Treatise of Human Nature*
Baron de Montesquieu	France	Government	Checks and balances; separation of powers	*The Spirit of the Laws*
Jean-Jacques Rousseau	France	Politics	Individual rights; the General Will	*The Social Contract*
Voltaire	France	Religion	Rationality; vehemently anti-religion	*Candide*
Immanuel Kant	Germany	Philosophy	Knowledge exists beyond reason	*Critique of Pure Reason*
Denis Diderot	France	Everything	Religious claims must fall under the domain of reason	*Encyclopédie*
Mary Wollstonecraft	England	Politics	Individual rights for women	*A Vindication of the Rights of Woman*
Cesare Beccaria	Italy	Politics	Individual rights for criminals	*On Crimes and Punishments*

The "Enlightened" Despots

The influence of these *philosophes* was felt far and wide, high and low. As a result, several European monarchs—who ruled over nations that were less progressive than England—were tempted to make gestures toward civil rights because it would centralize their own authority. These leaders have become known as the "enlightened" despots.

In Prussia, **Frederick William** reached an agreement with the landed nobility, the **Junkers**—he would recognize their ownership of the serfs if they provided him with tax money. His grandson, Frederick II (also known as **Frederick the Great**) was much more influenced by the *philosophes*. Disagreeing with his father, he freed the serfs (the ones living on public estates), limited the use of corporal punishment on those serfs, and ended all capital punishment.

In Austria, **Joseph II** issued the **Edicts of Toleration**, giving Jews, Lutherans, and Calvinists freedom of worship. This reduced the power of the Catholic Church in Austria—and increased his own. Joseph also abolished serfdom and forced nobles to start paying more taxes. After his death, his brother Leopold rolled back some of these radical ideas.

In Russia, **Peter the Great** attempted to drag his country into the Enlightenment by imitating Western European advances, particularly those of the French and the Dutch. He built a navy out of nothing, built a new city out of nothing and named it after himself (St. Petersburg), conquered new land, centralized commerce by monopolizing commodities, and instituted a meritocratic system of advancement in public service so that commoners could rise to rank of noble. A few years later, Catherine II—better known as **Catherine the Great**—dabbled in Enlightenment reform but ultimately dropped it when she realized it would reduce her own power. (More on them a little later in this chapter.)

In Spain, **Charles III** showed the influence of the *philosophes*. He decreased the number of clergy, feeling that they weren't contributing adequately to Spanish society. He modernized agriculture, promoted science and universities, and even tried to ban bullfighting.

Hot study tip: One easy way to remember the enlightened despots is that most of their countries end in *-ia* and most of their names end in *II*!

Who Are These People?

Too Many Fredericks

Prussia started out as three separate chunks of poor farmland full of poor peasants and poor nobles.

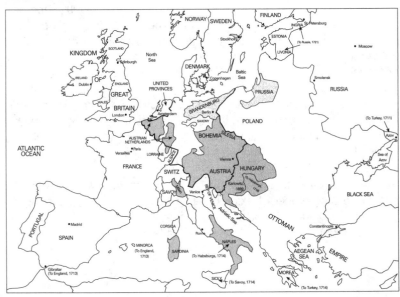

Europe in 1715

In 1640, **Frederick I** became Duke and decided Prussia needed a big army and efficient tax collectors. As mentioned before, he then made an alliance with the rural nobles, or **Junkers,** to make this happen, an alliance that would last over three hundred years. His son **Frederick William I** made himself a King, and his grandson **Frederick the Great** used the big army to steal Silesia from Maria Theresa. The Great Freddy loved philosophy and other fancy thoughts, palled around with Voltaire, and ended the death penalty in Prussia. He thought of himself as an **Enlightenment** ruler, and at his summer palace at Sanssouci (in French, "no worries") he wrote and discussed philosophy to relax.

Know Your Fredericks ❗	
Frederick	**Year**
Frederick William IV, the Great Elector	1640–1688
Duke Frederick III of Prussia	(1688–1701*)
King Frederick I of Prussia	1701–1713
Frederick William I	1713–1740
Frederick II, the Great	1740–1786

Who Shall Be Emperor? ❗

The Habsburg Empire under **Charles VI** was big but rickety, and that turned out to be a problem. He had no sons, and the Empire allowed only men to rule, so he spent the last 30 years of his rule trying to make sure that his oldest daughter, **Maria Theresa,** could rule after him. The piece of paper he got everybody to sign was called the **Pragmatic Sanction of 1713,** in which every major European power committed to recognizing Maria Theresa's right to the Habsburg throne. When he died in 1740, it turned out that pieces of paper weren't that important, and Maria Theresa had to fight a continental war for eight years before her rule was recognized. It would have been better for Charles to have perhaps recruited some soldiers, or saved some money, but he decided to go the "sign a piece of paper" route.

---

*Duke Frederick III of Prussia and King Frederick I of Prussia are actually the same Frederick!

Austria Creates Its Own Universe

Frederick the Great invaded **Austrian Silesia** post-haste after Charles died in 1740, supported by France and Spain. All three had signed the Pragmatic Sanction, but it seemed the opportunity was too good to pass up. Silesia was big and rich and well-populated, and Prussia was none of those things—in fact, Prussia, with two million inhabitants, was only about twice as big as Silesia alone, which had about a million. France and Spain were interested in stealing their own bits of Austria—France wanted the **Austrian Netherlands** while Spain wanted to reclaim hegemony over northern Italy—so Louis XV, Charles III of Spain, and Frederick II of Prussia decided to work together to take advantage of Maria Theresa's assumed weakness.

As it happened, Maria Theresa was not weak. She did come to the throne without much preparation, as her father, Charles VI Habsburg, avoided involving her in affairs of state before his death. She also came to the throne after her father had bankrupted the state through wars against France, Spain, and the Ottoman Empire. There were only 80,000 men in the Austrian Army, and they hadn't been paid in months since the treasury had the equivalent of a handful of nickels left after Charles's funeral. However, she learned quickly, and managed to persuade the Hungarians to contribute substantial funds and troops to defend her Empire.

Maria Theresa's Coronation as Queen of Hungary

The **Treaty of Breslau** in 1742 ended the **First Silesian War**, leaving Frederick in control of Silesia and Maria Theresa free to concentrate on France and Spain. Prussia re-entered the war in 1744 to make sure Maria Theresa didn't beat France too badly, and overran Bohemia in the **Second Silesian War**. The 1745 **Treaty of Dresden** again recognized Silesia as a Prussian possession, but Frederick recognized Maria Theresa's husband, **Francis**, as Holy Roman Emperor.

Once the initial spate of wars settled down, Maria Theresa set about working to reverse Frederick's seizure of Silesia. Her chief advisor, **Wenzel Anton**, undertook a diplomatic offensive that resulted in a realignment in European alliances. France switched from a Prussian to an Austrian ally, while Austria's traditional ally, Great Britain, began supporting Prussia as a check to Austria's new continental alliances. Domestically, she worked hard to strengthen and modernize the state apparatus. She expanded and rationalized taxation, including imposing some taxes on nobles and the clergy, resulting in state revenues doubling between 1754 and 1764. Much of the new revenue went to supporting a larger standing army of 108,000 men. She also began work on a new law code, the **Codex Theresianus**, in 1752, though it was not completed until 1766. This new code banned judicial torture and witch burning and expanded civil rights in Austria.

💬 Despite the extensive preparations, though, the **Seven Years' War** of 1756–1763 did not allow Austria to retake Silesia. Despite Frederick's tactical prowess, the weight of the French, Russian, and Austrian armies ground down his armies and by 1762 his position was dire. Austria had taken Silesia, while Russian armies occupied East Prussia and Pomerania, and it appeared as though Berlin would soon fall. However, the death of the Russian Empress Elizabeth and her replacement by **Peter III** led to a miracle. Peter was an ardent admirer of Frederick's philosophy and rule, and he not only refused to continue fighting against Prussia but actually switched sides, sending 18,000 men to defend Berlin. Though this alliance was shortlived, as Peter III was deposed and replaced by his wife, **Catherine II** (the Great) in July of 1762, Frederick used the time and support to rebuild his armies and strengthen his position. With all sides exhausted by the war, the 1763 **Treaty of Hubertusburg** restored the prewar status quo.

Soon after the extended conflict, Francis died, throwing Maria Theresa into mourning and bringing her son and heir, **Joseph II**, to the fore. Joseph replaced his father as Holy Roman Emperor and his mother named him co-ruler in 1765, though she remained the unquestioned final authority until her death in 1780. Joseph was an enlightened absolutist like Frederick II, and believed whole-heartedly in rational, secular government. Upon coming to power Joseph reformed and improved education, issued a **Patent of Toleration** granting a degree of religious freedom in Habsburg lands, abolished serfdom, ended censorship, and promoted use of the German language. However, many of these reforms created substantial opposition, and he was forced to withdraw many of them before his death in 1790.

Winter Is Coming

💬 Russia had largely been closed off from Western Europe during its time as the **Duchy of Muscovy**, feuding with the Mongol Horde and its neighboring Slavic realms. However, following the conquest of Novgorod and a number of Mongol Khanates under **Ivan the Terrible**, who ruled from 1533 to 1584, the Duchy of Muscovy became the Russian Empire. The death of the last member of Ivan's dynasty, Feodor, in 1598, however, ushered in chaos and war during what is now called the **Time of Troubles**. A series of coups and weak rulers attracted foreign invasion, extreme weather led to widespread famine, and Polish-Lithuanian troops in cooperation with Sweden invaded and occupied the country. A national uprising in late 1612 defeated and expelled the foreign occupiers and a grand assembly elected the young **Michael** Tsar in 1613, beginning the Romanov Dynasty.

❗ The Russian Empire became a European great power, though, under **Peter the Great**. Peter I Romanov came to the throne in 1682 as a modernizing absolutist fascinated by Western technology, industries, and fashions. This tendency was supercharged by his 18-month tour of Western Europe as part of a Russian **Grand Embassy**. He spent time studying urban planning in Britain and studying art in the Netherlands. He famously spent four months in the Netherlands working in the ship-yards there, learning techniques he would later use to help build the Russian Navy. Wherever he went, he also tried to hire as many experts and artisans as possible to send back to Russia.

He also partied a lot, and on one memorable occasion lost his lunch in a fountain in Brussels. A statue commemorates his great deed to this day.

Domestically, Peter was also an uncompromising Westernizer. He reorganized the Russian Army along Western European lines, invested heavily in making Russia a maritime power, and most famously decreed that nobles and soldiers must shave their beards and dress like French people.

Russian police would stop and shave people in the street if they couldn't produce a token to prove that they'd paid their beard tax. It wasn't cheap—this token cost a hundred rubles a year!

Peter the Great built St. Petersburg out of nothing to provide Russia a European-style capital as well as a Baltic port. He also put together the **Table of Ranks,** a hierarchy of nobility to codify authority and privilege.

❶ After several not particularly noteworthy Tsars and Tsarinas (Ivan VI, Elizabeth I, Peter III*) Russia was ruled by another great. **Catherine the Great**, a German princess, married Peter III, quickly overthrew him, and ruled for over 30 years (1762–1796). In foreign affairs, Catherine is primarily known for expanding Russia's territory. In the south, victories in wars against the Ottoman and Persian empires led to the seizure of what is now Ukraine and Azerbaijan, and made Russia the dominant power on the Black Sea. In Eastern Europe, Catherine put her old boyfriend **Stanislaw Poniatowski** on the throne of Poland-Lithuania and then turned it into a protectorate before the process reached its natural conclusion in the three partitions of Poland. Domestically, she continued the process of reform, introducing Enlightenment ideals to Russia in her **Nakaz**, a statement of legal principles meant to guide revisions to the Russian law code and reforming regional administration.

---

*These are the last three of six, plus one regent, between Peter the Great and Catherine the Great.

The Republic of Liberty 💬

What happened to Poland? As you might remember, the **Polish-Lithuanian Commonwealth** was the most powerful state in Europe during the Middle Ages, and invaded Muscovy and then Russia a number of times. However, while other European states underwent a centralizing process, strengthening the central government and improving tax collection, Poland-Lithuania went in the other direction. The Commonwealth's political foundation was the **Golden Liberty**, which functioned as a constitution. The substantial noble class elected the king directly, the parliament (the **Sejm**) essentially ruled the country, and the **Liberum Veto** enabled any individual member of the Sejm to veto legislation. It was certainly a great place to live at the time, and much freer than most places in Europe (in particular, religious tolerance was a thing there), but by the 17th century trouble was coming. The Sejm preferred to elect kings from outside of Poland-Lithuania to prevent them from strengthening the throne, which both embroiled the country in foreign politics and rendered their kings completely useless. Lack of revenue and political power prevented the creation of an efficient standing army (on purpose—armies were often used as tools of political repression!) leading to defeats in foreign wars. Finally, foreign powers found out that it was cheaper to bribe a nobleman to use the Liberum Veto to shut down the Sejm and prevent an army from being raised than it was to defeat one in the field. This was what led to Poland-Lithuania being ruled by Catherine's old boyfriend.

Actually, Stanislaw turned out to be a pretty good king, who tried to reform the government to make it more effective. In 1766, he sought to push a measure drastically restricting the Liberum Veto through the Sejm, which failed due to conservative and foreign opposition and led to a nasty semi-civil war followed by the **First Partition of Poland** in 1772. The Austrians, the Prussians, and the Russians took advantage of the disorder to seize some Polish territory. These seizures concentrated Polish minds, and in 1791 a new Polish Constitution was adopted. The **May Constitution** reformed the Commonwealth to produce a government similar to the British system at the time.

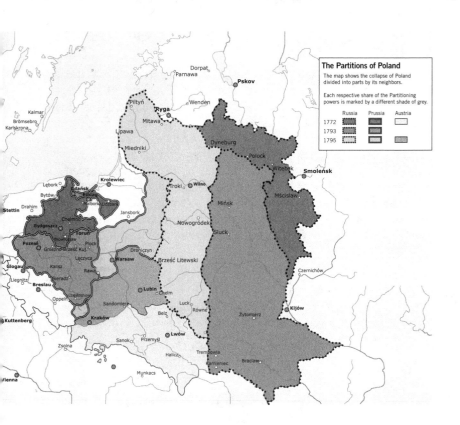

The Partitions of Poland

The map shows the collapse of Poland divided into parts by its neighbors.

Each respective share of the Partitioning powers is marked by a different shade of grey.

	Russia	Prussia	Austria
1772			
1793			
1795			

Polish conservatives, who saw this new constitution as a threat, allied themselves with the Russian Empire to overthrow it. A Russian invasion led to the **Second Partition of Poland**, in 1793. A patriotic uprising against the dismemberment of the country in 1794, the **Kosciuszko Uprising**, was eventually defeated by the Russians and in 1795 the three partition powers implemented the **Third Partition of Poland**, in which the country ceased to exist.

The Gold of the Americas ❗

The Spanish Empire had been significantly weakened by the **War of the Spanish Succession**, but remained involved in European affairs. Spain participated in the War of the Austrian Succession and the Seven Years' War, and **Charles III**'s ascension to the throne in 1759 brought Enlightened Absolutism to Spain. He reduced the power of the Catholic Church by expelling the Jesuits from Spain and seizing their assets, in what is known as the **Pragmatic Penalty** of 1767. He weakened the Inquisition, abolished antiquated legislation, and invested heavily in infrastructure development. During his reign Spain became more of a nation. In the colonies, he imposed slave codes to improve the economic efficiency of Spanish slave agriculture, though it remained a rolling horror.

Russia: Catherine the Great (1762–1796)
Enlightened influence: Montesquieu and Voltaire
Enlightened actions: systemized laws, brought ideas of French philosophy to Russian aristocracy

Prussia: Frederick II (the Great) (1740–1786)
Enlightened influence: Voltaire
Enlightened actions: freed the serfs, supported academia, ended capital punishment

Austria: Joseph II (1769–1790)
Enlightened influence: Voltaire
Enlightened actions: issued the Edicts of Toleration, weakened the Church

Spain: Charles III (1759–1788)
Enlightened influence: Benito Feijóo
Enlightened actions: weakened the Church, funded science and academia, kept peace

The Kingdom of Parliament 🔔

Following the English Civil War, the supremacy of Parliament was firmly established in Great Britain, and the Prime Minister changed from the King's agent to the effective head of government. Two political parties vied for control of Parliament—the Tories and the Whigs. The Whigs were pro-parliament and anti-Catholic, while the Tories were conservative, pro-aristocratic, and pro-royal. The most important reign for this period was that of **George III**, who presided over the Seven Years' War, the American Revolution, and the French Revolution. The expense of fighting the Seven Years' War drove Parliament to levy taxes on the American colonies, who then revolted with the help of the French in 1776 and eventually, in 1783, made their independence stick. The flexibility of the British civil service, the productivity of its factories, and its financial capacity allowed it to maintain control of the oceans during the Napoleonic Wars, fund a series of allies across six coalitions from 1789 to 1815, and emerge as the world's dominant power after Napoleon's defeat. Great Britain then became increasingly democratic, and the 1832 **Great Reform Act** in particular marked an important transition from an oligarchy of wealthier citizens to a more representative government by eliminating rotten boroughs and expanding the franchise to about 20% of the adult male population.

Whigs vs. Tories 🔔	
Whigs	**Tories**
• Supported the Church of England • Opposed the Catholic Church • Supported the Parliament and the gentry	• Supported the Crown • More sympathetic to Catholicism • Drew support from the Great Aristocrats

Galling Gallics ❗

The wars France fought against England and the expense of supporting the American Revolution significantly worsened France's internal problems. As you've read, the Bourbon Dynasty had made France the strongest power in Europe and conquered a substantial colonial empire. However, by the 1780s France had spent almost a century fighting major wars (with a period of peace from 1715 to 1740), and French participation in the American Revolution (1776–1783) had bankrupted the government. *Ancien Régime* (Old Order) France was actually poorly positioned to raise funds, though the country was quite rich. As a consequence of the nobility and the clergy being free of taxes, the common people were forced to pay all of the taxes and thus carried quite a heavy tax burden.

In 1788, **Louis XVI** needed money badly enough that he decided to tax the aristocracy. In order to do so, he needed permission—regional courts, called *parlements*, had veto power over new taxes. He'd tried to get past this in 1787 by calling an **Assembly of Notables**—a fancy way of saying getting a bunch of important people together. The body had no formal power, but the nobles assembled didn't want to pay taxes anyway, so that didn't work. For his next attempt he called a meeting of the **Estates-General**. This was a medieval-style gathering of all the people, in the form of the three Estates. The First Estate was the Church, the Second Estate was the nobility, and the **Third Estate** was literally everyone else. Elections were held for representatives in the spring of 1789, and 1200 representatives met in May 1789.

A French priest, the **Abbé Sieyès**, had written a pamphlet calling for the Third Estate to be given some power, instead of being crushed by the Church and the Nobles voting together, as typically happened. Why were the peasants so worked up? Well, the last several years in France had seen widespread food shortages and substantial increases in the price of grain, so there was a sense that reforms were needed. Enlightenment ideas had also undermined the legitimacy of royal absolutism and aristocratic privilege.

One way we know what people were upset about is the publication of hundreds of different **cahiers de doléances**, or books of complaint, which listed all the things people wanted to change!

So when the Estates-General met, the Third Estate in particular was eager to make a difference and willing to think in new ways to make it happen.

With the cooperation of the low-level clergy and some members of the gentry, the Third Estate gathered without the other two and, on June 17, voted themselves a **National Assembly**, a gathering of the people rather than of the estates. To keep the assembly from doing anything else crazy, Louis XVI closed the assembly hall, so everybody decamped to a tennis court and swore the **Tennis Court Oath**, which bound them to provide France a constitution before they closed the assembly. The King began moving troops, many of them foreign mercenaries, into Paris, and that's when the mob intervened.

The population of Paris went nuts, with riots, looting, and mob violence against aristocratic and royal targets more or less in support of the National Assembly. Some French army personnel also went over to the popular uprising, and on July 14, 1789, a mob stormed the **Bastille** fortress in Paris to seize the arms and ammunition stored there. The common people of Paris organized themselves into the **Paris Commune**, a radical civil organization.

The Storming of the Bastille by Jean-Pierre Houël

Popular uprisings against aristocratic privilege started to spread across France, and peasant militias looted and burned manor houses. This phase of the revolution, called the **Great Fear**, drove thousands of nobles to flee France and signaled the collapse of the old order. By the late summer of 1789, power was in the hands of the National Assembly (insofar as anyone was in charge) and a National Guard was created, commanded by **Marquis de Lafayette**, the hero of the American Revolution.

The Assembly released a statement of its principles in August, the ***Declaration of the Rights of Man and Citizen***, which argued that political rights belonged to the people rather than the King and that all men were equal (the men of the National Assembly were way less interested in the equality of women).

Did You Know?

Women in France were not thrilled about being left out of the whole rights thing. Olympe de Gouges, for one, argued that women were also people and citizens with rights in her *Declaration of the Rights of Woman and the Female Citizen,* but it would take a bit more than a century for this argument to bear fruit.

During this period, the King and his family were moved to Paris so that the National Assembly could keep an eye on him. The new constitution, drafted by 1791, gave France a single legislative chamber with the King as a figurehead.

France's colonies took note of the Declaration as well, with the most important colonial consequence being the **Haitian Revolution** of 1791. The ex-slave Toussaint L'Ouverture cooperated with other free people of color and in tandem with a widespread slave revolt to throw off the yoke of slaveholders and eventually to win independence for Haiti in 1804.

During this period, known as the Constitutional Monarchy, the National Assembly implemented substantial reforms changing how the state was organized (dividing the country into 83 equally sized departments), abolished the privileges of the Catholic Church, and abolished slavery. The new government seized all Church property in France to pay for the French debt, and the 1790 **Civil Constitution of the Clergy** declared that clergy were now employees of the state, though only about 20 percent agreed to it. The rest went into hiding, exile, or prison, rousing opposition to the new order. One such opponent was King Louis XVI, who fled Paris in 1791 in an attempt to reach royalist military forces on the Eastern border of France. He was eventually recognized and arrested before the royal family reached their goal, and once returned to Paris they were placed under arrest in the palace. This was a key moment in the radicalization of the French Revolution. Soon after, the National Assembly disbanded and was replaced by the elected Legislative Assembly, which would govern France from October 1791 to September 1792.

The main factions were the Jacobins, who were more radical and, at the time, a minority, and the Girondins, who mostly ran things and were more moderate. The Jacobins sat on the left side of the Parliament, up on the highest seats (on "the Mountain") while the Girondins sat on the right. Between them were the unaligned (centrist) deputies, who sat in the big flat part ("the Plain"). The Jacobins were the party of the urban poor, and were consequently much more radical. They supported expanding the franchise to every male French adult, supported government intervention in the economy to guarantee everyone food, and were opposed to wealth, privilege, and religion. Their main opponents, the Girondins, were, generally speaking, moderates who drew their support from shopkeepers, merchants, and other citizens of means. The Girondins supported free trade, protections for property and wealth, and a limited franchise in which you had to pay some taxes in order to be able to vote.

 Did You Know?

This is why we still use "left" and "right" when talking about politics.

Jacobins vs. Girondins ❗	
Jacobins	**Girondins**
• Radicals supported by the urban poor • Supported price ceilings for bread • Supported giving the vote to every Frenchman	• Moderates supported by the bourgeoisie • Supported a free market economy • Supported giving the vote to rich men

Foreign monarchs were quite upset by this whole revolution thing, and Austrian and Prussian armies showed up on the French border as they tried to figure out what to do. The Girondin faction that led the Legislative Assembly thought that a quick successful war would strengthen support for the revolution and thus declared war in April

1792, quickly defeating the invading Prussians and overrunning the Austrian Netherlands. However, domestic chaos and royal opposition to the Constitution led to a constitutional crisis. A new **Convention** was elected under universal male suffrage to write a new constitution. The Convention first met on September 20, 1792, and immediately abolished the monarchy and declared a Republic.

European opinion was not completely negative, though! There was substantial sympathy in Britain for the French Revolution during its early years, since Britain was a strong believer in parliamentary accountability. **William Pitt the Younger**, George III's longest-serving Prime Minister, for example, thought there was potential until the Convention period. His Whig rival, **Charles Fox**, felt similarly. **Edmund Burke**, though, the famous conservative theorist, opposed the Revolution on grounds of its excessive radicalism.

⬤⬤⬤ The Convention further radicalized the Revolution, and after evidence was found linking Louis XVI to cooperation with foreign powers, he was put on trial, sentenced to death, and executed on January 21, 1793. This whole revolution thing didn't sit well with the French nobility; many French nobles tried to flee, but many in the west of France tried to overthrow the revolution. This uprising was called the *Vendée*, after the region it started in, and Louis's execution was the last straw for the nobles there. This uprising, beginning in March 1793, was eventually crushed, but it coincided with defeats against foreign armies abroad in the summer of 1793 and price increases in the cities to lead to a Jacobin coup against the Girondist leadership of the Convention. The Paris mob, composed of the *Sans-Culottes* (literally "the pantsless," who were too poor to buy fancy pants) enabled the **Committee of Public Safety**, charged with safeguarding the revolution, to seize dictatorial powers. The Committee, led by **Maximilien Robespierre**, arrested, imprisoned, and guillotined over 40,000 people accused of counter-revolutionary activities, which could basically mean anything. This era is known as the **Reign of Terror**.

👀 During this period, Revolutionary policy also radicalized. The **Law of the Maximum**, passed in September 1793, established price ceilings for grain, flour, meat, soap, firewood, and some other goods so that these would remain affordable for the common people. Practically speaking, this meant hoarding and shortages. Lazare Carnot implemented a *Levée en Masse*, a policy whereby the entire population was mobilized to either join the army or produce for the war effort. Catholicism was abolished and replaced first by the secular **Cult of Reason** and, when that proved incredibly unpopular, by the Deist **Cult of the Supreme Being**. The overall goal for Robespierre was to create a **Republic of Virtue**, where every citizen embodied liberty, brotherhood, and egalitarianism.

Charles-André Merda Shooting Robespierre by Jean-Joseph-François Tassert

It didn't quite work out. In July 1794, Robespierre's time ran out—enough people had gotten sick of living in terror to break his hold on the Convention. The **Thermidorean Reaction**—a backlash against Robespierre and the Jacobins—ushered Robespierre to the same guillotine he had sent so many others to.

❗ The end of the Committee discredited the convention, and led to the creation of another new government in 1795, the **Directory**, along with a third constitution. Though this came about as a reaction against the Terror, the Directory moved aggressively to jail, execute, and exile its enemies among the Jacobins in what is called the **White Terror**. However, living standards didn't really improve that much, and the Directory put its hope for public appeal and into military success.

❗ Military success there was. The *levée,* en masse, provided the manpower and material to overpower the small cabinet armies of the other European powers. Revolutionary armies defeated Prussia and Spain in 1795, replacing the Dutch Republic with a puppet Republic. In 1796, fighting in the Holy Roman Empire was inconclusive, but a Corsican general named **Napoleon Bonaparte** took charge of the Italian campaign, driving multiple Austrian armies out of the peninsula in a daring campaign, which opened Vienna to invasion and drove the Habsburgs to sign a peace treaty in 1797. The only country that remained at war with France at this point was Great Britain, and after much of the *ancien régime* navy went over to Britain during the Revolution, there wasn't any good way to attack Britain proper. So Napoleon invaded Egypt, which was then a British possession. He took the country, but a British fleet under Admiral Horatio Nelson sank the French fleet supporting Napoleon in 1798, trapping his army in Egypt.

Napoleon evaded the British blockade and returned to Paris in 1799, there to join with a handful of leading Directory figures to launch a *coup d'état* against the widely despised Directory in 1799. This fourth constitution made Napoleon the **First Consul** for 10 years—in essence, a dictator. In this phase of his rule, he signed a **Concordat** with Pope Pius VII in 1801 regularizing the French state's relationship with the Catholic Church. Though the arrangement was not as severe as that of the Civil Constitution, Napoleon reserved the right to appoint French Bishops and to supervise Church finances in France. In 1802, a new plebiscite was held to revise the constitution and make Napoleon First Consul for life, and in 1804 another vote made him Emperor. As Emperor, he established a uniform law code, the **Napoleonic Code**, which drastically revised and modernized French law along lines that are still used today.

Though Napoleon's domestic reforms were important, it was his campaigns of conquest that threw Europe into turmoil. Britain, Russia, and Austria joined together in the Third Coalition in 1805, in which Napoleon destroyed Austrian and Russian armies at **Austerlitz** after sacking Vienna, forcing a peace and leaving France the master of the continent. However, Admiral Nelson returned to the picture and, at the **Battle of Trafalgar** in late 1805, obliterated Napoleon's hope of matching Britain at sea. Prussia declared war in 1806 after France established the Confederation of the Rhine, an assortment of smaller German states now essentially French puppets, threatening Prussian influence in the Holy Roman Empire. The Fourth Coalition, including Britain, Russia, and Prussia, set out to check Napoleon but failed again, as Napoleon shattered the Prussian army at the battles of **Jena and Auerstedt** in 1806 before Russia could mobilize, sacked Berlin, and defeated the Russian Army in 1807 at the **Battle of Friedland**. The **Treaty of Tilsit**, which ended the war of the Fourth Coalition, gutted Prussia, and turned much of Russian Poland into the puppet **Duchy of Warsaw**.

💬 Though Napoleon continued to succeed in Continental Europe, he lacked a good way to knock Britain out of the war. Defeating Britain's continental allies was one approach, but at this point he'd tried that a number of times, so he decided to set up what he called his **Continental System**. This was a law forbidding trade with Britain, and after the Treaty of Tilsit, he had forced all of Europe to agree to it. In practice, this ended up hurting the European economies more than it did Britain's, and there was widespread black market trade with Britain. One of the biggest offenders was the Kingdom of Portugal, and in 1807 Napoleon sent an army to put a stop to it. The next year, he invaded Spain and put his brother, Joseph Bonaparte, on the Spanish throne. This began the **Peninsular War**, which tied down hundreds of thousands of French soldiers in a brutal guerilla war against Spanish insurgents. In 1809, a British expeditionary force under the Duke of Wellington landed in Portugal in support of the guerrillas and eventually drove the French off the Peninsula. Austria sought to re-enter the war in 1809 as well, in cooperation with the British, but after a series of brutal battles in Germany, Napoleon once again sacked Vienna and forced a peace.

And for a few years, there was peace in Europe, but in 1812 Russia's forced acquiescence to the Continental system was cracking and Napoleon set out to destroy Russian power. He gathered together a *Grande Armée* of over a half million soldiers and invaded Russia on June 24, 1812. Though when the Russian Army stood and fought (such as at Smolensk and Borodino), Napoleon managed to eke out victories. The Russian strategy was to exhaust and starve the French Army by executing a scorched-earth withdrawal into the Russian interior. Napoleon's strategy was to force a decisive battle and conclude a peace, so Tsar Alexander's withdrawals left him in a pickle. The French were getting cold and hungry, so they launched an attack on Moscow to seize food and shelter for the winter. Napoleon defeated the Russians and took the city, but before withdrawing, Alexander ordered the city burned to the ground. Napoleon and his *Grande Armée* had to retreat, decimated by cold and hunger—only 27,000 French soldiers made it out of Russia alive.

❗ This was a key moment in the Napoleonic Wars, and his defeat in Russia brought Prussia and Austria back into the war, joining with Russia, Britain, Spain, and Portugal to form the Sixth Coalition. Though Napoleon managed to win some battles, he lost control of his German territories after the 1813 **Battle of Leipzig**. Napoleon refused allied peace terms, and so by 1814 the coalition invaded France. Paris surrendered in March 1814, and Napoleon recognized reality and abdicated in April.

The Hundred Days!

The first time Napoleon was exiled to Elba Island, he escaped, returned to Paris, and raised an army. Louis XVIII ran away as fast as possible, and Napoleon was Emperor once more. Unfortunately, everybody else was super-sick of wars against Napoleon, so they sent armies ASAP and defeated Napoleon at **Waterloo**, in 1815. They then picked a much more distant island for Napoleon to live, St. Helena, where he died.

Rebalancing Europe ❗

In response to the decade of chaos, **Prince Metternich** of Austria called all European powers to the **Congress of Vienna** in 1814. There, he— along with Russia, Prussia, and England—decided that they needed to do two things post-Napoleon. One, they wanted to keep order by keeping France down. To do that, they reinstituted the Bourbon monarchy. Two, they needed to repress liberalism and nationalism, which they did by refusing cries for Poland's return.

Metternich and the conservative policies set at the Congress of Vienna would dominate the social order of Europe for the next 35 years. Their iron grip ended only when the revolutionary spirit of liberalism and nationalism had spread so far and so loudly across the continent that change could no longer be denied.

Year(s)	Event
1648	Peace of Westphalia
1648	Beginning of the Fronde
1649	Execution of Charles I and establishment of English republic
1651	Thomas Hobbes publishes *Leviathan*
1653	Oliver Cromwell becomes Lord Protector
1658	Death of Cromwell
1660	Restoration of Charles II
1661	Death of Cardinal Mazarin; Louis XIV becomes his own chief minister
1661	Louis XIV begins construction of the Palace of Versailles
1662	Royal Society charter granted by Charles II
1664	Chartering of the French East India Company
1670	Posthumous publication of Pascal's *Pensées*
1682	Beginning of the reign of Peter the Great
1685	Revocation of the Edict of Nantes
1685	James II, a Catholic, becomes King of England
1687	Newton publishes his *Principia*
1688	Glorious Revolution
1689	John Locke's *Two Treatises of Government*

Year(s)	Event
1689	Act of Toleration
1690	John Locke's *An Essay Concerning Human Understanding*
1701	Prussia becomes a kingdom
1701	Act of Settlement passed to bypass potential Catholic kings
1703	Cornerstone laid for the new city of St. Petersburg
1707	Acts of Union bring about political unification of England and Scotland
1713	Treaty of Utrecht marks the end of the War of the Spanish Succession
1714	George I becomes first Hanoverian King of England
1721	End of the Great Northern War between Russia and Sweden
1721	Start of Robert Walpole's tenure as prime minister
1739	Hume's *A Treatise of Human Nature*
1740	Frederick the Great becomes King of Prussia
1740	Start of the War of the Austrian Succession
1746	Battle of Culloden
1748	Montesquieu's *The Spirit of Laws*
1748	Treaty of Aix-la-Chapelle marks the end of War of the Austrian Succession

Year(s)	Event
1751	The first volume of Diderot's *Encyclopédie* appears
1755	Lisbon earthquake
1756	Maria Theresa carries out the "Diplomatic Revolution"
1756	Beginning of the Seven Years' War
1759	Voltaire's *Candide*
1762	Rousseau's *The Social Contract*
1762	Rousseau's *Émile* is published
1762	Start of the reign of Catherine the Great
1763	Voltaire pushes for reexamination in the trial of Jean Calas
1763	Treaty of Paris marks the end of the Seven Years' War
1764	Beccaria's *On Crime and Punishments*
1765	Stamp Act
1770	Burke writes *Thoughts on the Cause of the Present Discontents*
1770	Marriage of the future Louis XVI to Marie Antoinette
1774	Louis XVI becomes King of France
1774	First Continental Congress
1775	Fighting begins between American colonists and British
1776	Jefferson writes the Declaration of Independence

Year(s)	Event
1776	The first volume of Edward Gibbon's *The History of the Decline and Fall of the Roman Empire* is published
1776	Adam Smith's *The Wealth of Nations*
1778	France goes to war against Britain in support of the American colonies
1781	Kant's *Critique of Pure Reason*
1781	Joseph II of Austria issues Edicts of Toleration
1786	Calonne, finance minister to Louis XVI, informs him that the crown is bankrupt
1787	Assembly of Notables meets
1789	Louis XVI decides to call the Estates-General
1789	Abbé Sieyès writes *What Is the Third Estate?*
1789	Estates-General meets for the first time (May 5)
1789	Third Estate declares that they will meet only as a National Assembly (June 17)
1789	Tennis Court Oath (June 20)
1789	Storming of the Bastille (July 14)
1789	Lafayette selected as commander of the National Guard
1789	Great Fear (July–August)
1789	Renunciation of aristocratic privileges (August 4)

Year(s)	Event
1789	*Declaration of the Rights of the Man and of the Citizen of 1789* is adopted by the Constituent Assembly (August 27)
1789	Women's march on Versailles (October 5)
1789	Jeremy Bentham's *An Introduction to the Principles of Morals and Legislation*
1790	Civil Constitution of the Clergy
1790	Edmund Burke's *Reflections on the Revolution in France*
1791	Constitution adopted
1791	Revolt breaks out in French colony of St. Domingue
1791	Louis XVI attempts to flee Paris (June 21)
1792	Mary Wollstonecraft's *A Vindication of the Rights of Woman*
1792	France declares war on Austria (April 20)
1792	Mob of *sans-culottes* storms the Tuileries Palace (August 10)
1792	September Massacres
1792	Battle of Valmy (September 20)
1792	France becomes a republic (September 22)
1793	Execution of Louis XVI (January 21)
1793	Universal conscription for the French armies begins (February 24)
1793	Execution of Marie Antoinette (October 16)
1793	Britain enters the war against France

Year(s)	Event
1793	Counter-revolution breaks out in the Vendée (March)
1793	Establishment of the Committee of Public Safety (April)
1793	Expulsion of Girondins from the Convention (June 2)
1793	Ratification of new republican constitution (June 24)
1793	Charlotte Corday murders Marat (July 13)
1793	Napoleon retakes Toulon from counter-revolutionaries
1794	Execution of Georges Danton (April 5)
1794	Festival of the Supreme Being (June 8)
1794	Fall of Robespierre and the Jacobins (July 27)
1795	Establishment of the Directory
1795	Napoleon puts down royalist revolt (October 5)
1796	Napoleon launches invasion of northern Italy
1798	Napoleon begins invasion of Egypt
1798	French fleet defeated at the Battle of the Nile (August)
1798	Thomas Malthus's *An Essay on the Principle of Population*
1799	Napoleon involved in coup overthrowing Directory
1799	Napoleon becomes First Consul
1801	Napoleon and Pope Pius VII sign concordat

Year(s)	Event
1802	Plebiscite establishes Napoleon as Consul for Life
1802	Treaty of Amiens between Britain and France
1803	Napoleon sells Louisiana Territory to the United States
1804	Napoleon crowned Emperor
1804	Execution of the Duke of Enghien
1804	Promulgation of the Civil Code
1804	Formation of the Third Coalition
1805	British victory over French-Spanish fleet at Trafalgar
1805	Defeat of the Austrians and Russians at Austerlitz
1806	Defeat of the Prussians at the Battle of Jena
1806	Abolition of the Holy Roman Empire
1806	Continental System implemented
1807	Napoleon and Alexander I sign Treaty of Tilsit
1807	Spain and France invade Portugal
1807	British Parliament votes for the end of the slave trade
1807	First passenger train line
1812	Napoleon's invasion of Russia
1812	Occupation of Moscow (September)

Year(s)	Event
1813	Retreat from Russia
1813	Battle of Leipzig (October)
1814	Napoleon forced to abdicate and the reign of Louis XVIII begins
1814	Congress of Vienna convenes (September)
1815	Napoleon escapes from Elba (February 26)
1815	Battle of Waterloo marks end of the Hundred Days (June 18)
1815	Napoleon sent into exile on St. Helena

CHAPTER 3

Age of Revolutions to World War I:
c. 1815–c. 1914

Restoration and Revolution

Following the final fall of Napoleon in 1815 and the restoration of the Bourbons to the throne of France, the rulers of Europe were faced with a daunting task—restoring stability to the relationships between the nations of Europe while also ensuring that the specter of revolution did not reappear within their domains.

Many European nations attempted to control their populations by copying methods used by France

Larger and more efficient bureacracies

Secret police forces

More efficient censorship offices

In an undeveloped nation such as Russia, these oppressive institutions were the only well-functioning part of the state.

Public Enemy #1: The Enlightenment 💬

European states attributed much of the war and chaos of the Napoleonic years to the Enlightenment. They strived to reverse the effects of the Enlightenment by promoting the institution most injured by it: religion.

The Anglican clergy worked in the House of Lords to block parliamentary measures such as the bill in favor of Catholic emancipation and the Great Reform Bill.

England

The Orthodox clergy remained a bulwark of the reactionary policies of the state.

Russia

The Inquisition was once again allowed to operate following its disappearance during the Napoleonic domination of Spain.

Spain

An Age of Competing Ideologies 🔊

The Restoration period that followed the French Revolution was characterized by competing ideologies that were rooted either in support for the French Revolution or approbation of it. The competing ideologies ranged from a commitment to the restored order that emerged after 1815 to calls for its demise.

Ideology	Conservatism	Nationalism	Liberalism	Utopian Socialism
View on revolution	Opposes radical revolution; believes in the possibility of slow political change over the passage of time	May advocate revolution when the governing authorities no longer act in the interest of the national identity	Revolution is necessary to defend the **individual's natural rights.**	A number of radical Jacobins saw revolution as necessary to achieve economic equality for all through the common ownership of all property.
Notable thinker	**Edmund Burke**, a member of the English House of Commons	🔊 German philosopher **Johann Gottfried Herder** is credited with coining the term *nationalism*.	**John Locke**	🔊 **Henri de Saint-Simon** (1760–1825) argued that the creation of a hierarchical society led by an intellectual class would improve society.

Ideology	Conservatism	Nationalism	Liberalism	Utopian Socialism
Key text	*Reflections on the Revolution in France* (1790)	🔊 While there was no single key text, in places such as Germany, writers such as the **Grimm brothers** recorded old German folktales to reveal a traditional German national spirit that was part of a common past, whether one lived in Bavaria, Saxony, or any of the other German states.	Lafayette's *Declaration of the Rights of Man*	🔊 *A New View of Society* (1813) by **Robert Owen**, who actually created a living, breathing utopian socialist community in a Scottish mill town known as New Lanark
Core beliefs	• The principle of the rights of man and natural law is fundamentally dangerous to the social order. • Tradition is the basic underpinning for the rights of those in positions of authority.	• People's identities are defined by their connection with a nation and it is to this nation that they owe their primary loyalty as opposed to their king or local lord. • Common national identities stem from shared history, language, religion, ethnicity, social practices, and ancestors, among a multitude of other factors.	• Support for limits on political authorities through the writing of **constitutions** and the formation of **parliamentary bodies** • Emphasizes the individual's right to enjoy religious freedom, freedom of the press, and equality under the law	• Capitalism over-emphasized production, under-emphasized distribution, and possessed other serious flaws such as unemployment and the suffering brought about by low wages. • Expansive possibilities are available to mankind; poor environments corrupted human nature.

Ideology	Conservatism	Nationalism	Liberalism	Utopian Socialism
Taking it to the extreme	〰 **Joseph de Maistre** (1753–1821), an *émigré* during the French Revolution, argued for the Church's supreme authority in delegating political authority, and that monarchs should not tolerate those who advocated even the slightest degree of political reform.	💬 In the German and Italian states, the desire to rid their lands of French soldiers created a unifying purpose that helped establish a national identity. Pan-Slavism united Slavic-speaking peoples under a common identity.	Liberalism was connected to the events of the early stages of the French Revolution with the establishment of the constitutional monarchy.	〰 **Charles Fourier** (1772–1837) made a blueprint for a cooperative community, which consisted of a self-contained group of people rotating the labor tasks. Fourier thought that because children liked to play with dirt, they should take care of the community's garbage.

Nationalism emerged as an important ideology during the French Revolution. At this time, developments like national conscription, the calling of all young men for military service, helped create the idea of a citizen whose primary loyalty lies not to a village or province but to the nation instead.

Early 19th-century nationalism was often, though not exclusively, tied to liberalism because many nationalists, like the liberals, wanted political equality and human freedom to serve as the bedrock for the new state.

ASAP European History

Liberalism as an Economic Theory ❗

Besides being a political theory, liberalism was also a school of economic thought. The most important of the early liberal economists—individuals who collectively formed what became known as the **classical school**—was **Adam Smith** (1723–1790), who published his most important work, *An Inquiry into the Nature and Causes of the Wealth of Nations*, in 1776.

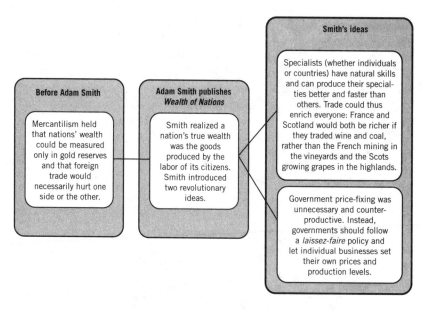

Before Adam Smith

Mercantilism held that nations' wealth could be measured only in gold reserves and that foreign trade would necessarily hurt one side or the other.

Adam Smith publishes Wealth of Nations

Smith realized a nation's true wealth was the goods produced by the labor of its citizens. Smith introduced two revolutionary ideas.

Smith's ideas

Specialists (whether individuals or countries) have natural skills and can produce their specialties better and faster than others. Trade could thus enrich everyone: France and Scotland would both be richer if they traded wine and coal, rather than the French mining in the vineyards and the Scots growing grapes in the highlands.

Government price-fixing was unnecessary and counterproductive. Instead, governments should follow a *laissez-faire* policy and let individual businesses set their own prices and production levels.

Smith argued that individual decisions, as though guided by an "**invisible hand**," would provide a balance between supply and demand, while also providing businesses an incentive to find cheaper ways to produce more goods, lower prices, and increase sales.

18th-century French economists actually laid the groundwork for Smith's ideas. François Quesnay and Anne Robert Jacques Turgot argued against mercantilism by suggesting that a nation's wealth is derived from land development and agricultural potential. In that sense, they made a revolutionary claim that the value of a nation's wealth is tied directly to productive labor. Advocates of this economic theory in France were known as **Physiocrats**.

The Dismal Science 💬

Economics is sometimes referred to as "the dismal science" because the classical economists reached conclusions that can only be viewed as deeply depressing.

"It has appeared that from the inevitable laws of our nature, some human beings must suffer from want. These are the unhappy persons who, in the great lottery of life, have drawn a blank."
—*An Essay on the Principle of Population* (1798)

Thomas Malthus (1766–1834)

Malthus saw population growth as a problem that would one day outpace the food supply.

"Labor, like all other things which are purchased and sold, and which may be increased or diminished in quantity, has its natural and its market price."
—*On the Principles of Political Economy and Taxation* (1817)

David Ricardo (1772–1823)

Ricardo claimed that, according to the "**Iron Law of Wages**," as the number of workers increases, wages would inevitably continue to decrease.

Malthus and Ricardo were both writing at a time when the dramatic expansion of production brought on by the Industrial Revolution was making their negative predictions obsolete.

"State"ing the Obvious? 💬

Some writers, although we still apply to them the label of "liberal," began to question certain classical, liberal orthodoxies on the workings of the economy as well as the role of the state.

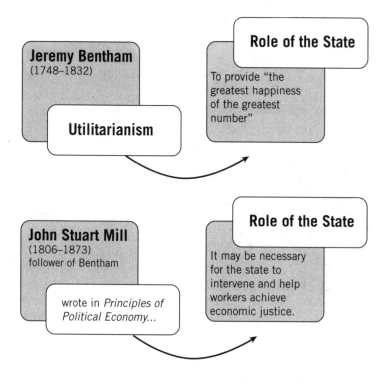

In the past, the struggle for liberty involved placing constraints on monarchs. However, Mill saw a feature of democratic governments as the danger of his time period: the majority could deny liberty to the minority. Accordingly, in some of Mill's later works, he began to move into a direction that brought him ever closer to socialism.

On Liberty

John Stuart Mill (1859)

- Questioned the absolute right to hold private property
- Claimed that there needed to be a more equitable way for societies to distribute their wealth

Did You Know?

 Unlike other male liberals who saw political liberty solely as a male domain, Mill was greatly influenced by the feminist thought of his wife, **Harriet Taylor Mill** (1807–1858). Inspired by her, he wrote *The Subjection of Women,* arguing in favor of granting full equality to women.

Ask Yourself...

- To what extent was the Napoleonic era responsible for the emergence of each of the new ideologies at the dawn of the 19th century?
- Which ideology from the 19th century had the most lasting impact? Which had the least impact? Why?

Political Restoration and Reform

The term *restoration* literally refers to the events in France during which the Bourbons were restored to the throne following the final defeat of Napoleon at Waterloo. The return to royal power was marked by several significant events:

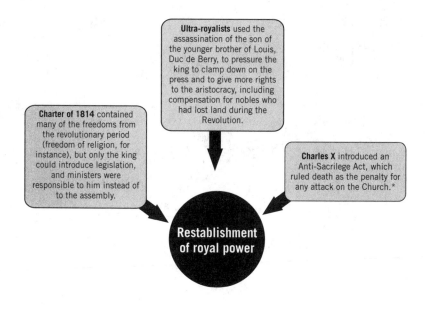

Ultra-royalists used the assassination of the son of the younger brother of Louis, Duc de Berry, to pressure the king to clamp down on the press and to give more rights to the aristocracy, including compensation for nobles who had lost land during the Revolution.

Charter of 1814 contained many of the freedoms from the revolutionary period (freedom of religion, for instance), but only the king could introduce legislation, and ministers were responsible to him instead of to the assembly.

Charles X introduced an Anti-Sacrilege Act, which ruled death as the penalty for any attack on the Church.*

Restablishment of royal power

  Did You Know?

Ultra-royalists were individuals who wanted to see the revival of absolute monarchy.

---

*This act was never applied, except on one minor point.

Restoration Monarchs to Know

Louis XVIII
- (1755–1824)
- Younger brother of Louis XVI
- In 1814, became first monarch of France since 1789

Charles X
- (1757–1836)
- More bitter about the Revolution than was his brother Louis XVIII
- In 1829, Charles appointed the Prince of Polignac as his chief minister, a man disliked throughout the country for being a leading ultra-royalist.

July, July! ❗

By 1830, the Prince of Polignac issued what became known as the **July Ordinances,** which dissolved the newly elected assembly, took away the right to vote from the upper bourgeoisie, and imposed rigid censorship. In response, frustrated liberals launched a revolution in Paris. Liberal leaders were cautious about the direction a new revolution could take:

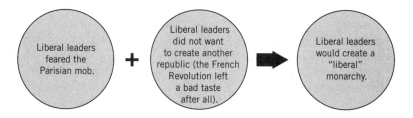

Liberal leaders feared the Parisian mob. **+** Liberal leaders did not want to create another republic (the French Revolution left a bad taste after all). **➡** Liberal leaders would create a "liberal" monarchy.

The **July Revolution** of 1830 ended with the crowning of Louis Philippe, the Duke of Orleans, and the creation of what became known as the **July monarchy**.

 ## *Did You Know?*

 The 1830 July Revolution sparked revolutions throughout Europe.

You Say You Want a Revolution

By the third decade of the 19th century, people across Europe showed signs that it would be impossible to stem their desire for change.

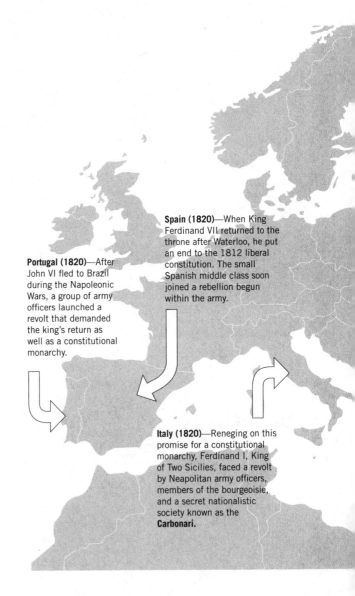

Portugal (1820)—After John VI fled to Brazil during the Napoleonic Wars, a group of army officers launched a revolt that demanded the king's return as well as a constitutional monarchy.

Spain (1820)—When King Ferdinand VII returned to the throne after Waterloo, he put an end to the 1812 liberal constitution. The small Spanish middle class soon joined a rebellion begun within the army.

Italy (1820)—Reneging on this promise for a constitutional monarchy, Ferdinand I, King of Two Sicilies, faced a revolt by Neapolitan army officers, members of the bourgeoisie, and a secret nationalistic society known as the **Carbonari.**

Serbia (1830)—Breaking off from the Ottoman Empire with a revolutionary movement, **Serbians** created a small kingdom on the southern border of the Austro-Hungarian Empire, which strongly promoted nationalism in the Balkan regions of Austria.

Greece (1821)—Hoping to see their ideas spread across the continent, Western European liberals looked to the Greek independence movement against Ottoman rule. With assistance from British, French, and Russian naval forces (as well as some cash from British Romantic poet **Lord Byron**), Greece declared its independence in 1832, becoming a monarchy with an imported Bavarian prince.

Did You Know?

The Greek revolt was also tied to what became known as the "**Eastern Question**"—what should be done about the increasingly weak Ottoman Empire, appropriately nicknamed "**the Sick Man of Europe**." Like other multiethnic empires, the Ottoman Empire was breaking down after a series of rulers who could not keep the groups united.

Although King Ferdinand of Spain agreed to rule under the laws of the constitution to end the rebellion, Austria, France, Prussia, and Russia wanted to intervene to stem the tide of revolutions throughout Europe. The British, however, refused to directly intervene; they did not want the five great powers of Europe to be involved in putting down internal rebellions in other nations. Two years later, a French army acted unilaterally—although with the tacit support of Russia, Prussia, and Austria—and restored Ferdinand to absolute power.

Similarly, during the revolt in Naples, Metternich wanted the support of the other great powers, so he called the rulers of Austria, Prussia, and Russia to the Austrian town of Troppau to create what became the **Troppau Protocol,** which stated that the great European powers had the right to intervene in revolutionary situations. The following year, the rebellion in Naples was put down with the help of Austrian troops.

Two Exceptions to the Rule ❶

For completely different reasons, Great Britain and Russia did not see prolonged periods of revolution. In both cases, attempts at revolution were met with brutal violence from the government. Great Britain, however, ultimately saw the dawn of liberal reforms, not through revolution, but through normal parliamentary processes.

Great Britain	Russia

Peterloo Massacre
- 1819: a crowd of 60,000 people gathered in St. Peter's field in Manchester to demand fundamental political changes, including universal male suffrage and annual parliaments
- Soldiers on hand shot eleven members of the crowd
- Parliament passed the **Six Acts,** which banned demonstrations and imposed censorship

Liberal Reform
Seeing the inevitability of change, Parliament passed a series of reforms to avoid further risk of revolution:
- 1824: repeal of **Combination Acts,** which had banned unions
- 1832: **Great Reform Bill** expanded voting rights (if only ever so slightly)
- 1833: slavery is banned in he British Empire and the **Factory Act** reduced the amount of hours children could work

Alexander I
(r. 1801–1825) at various times had toyed with the idea of political reform, although grew increasingly reactionary in later years

Following Alexander's death, a group known as the **Decembrists** staged a coup to install Constantine as tsar, a man who they (incorrectly) thought favored liberal reform

Nicholas I
(r. 1825–1855) became emperor when Constantine turned down the throne

Violently quashed the **Decembrist revolt** and strictly forbade further reform movements

 Did You Know?

Not all reforms benefited the working class: the **Poor Law of 1834** forced the destitute to enter into workhouses where conditions were purposefully miserable to discourage people from seeking assistance.

Other British Reforms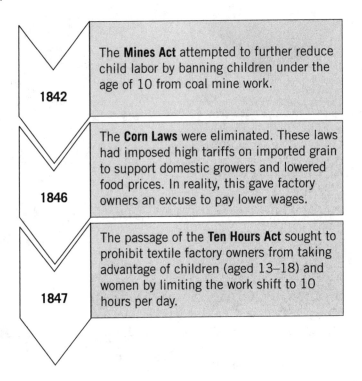

There are a few reforms from the 1840s that you may want to be aware of:

1842
The **Mines Act** attempted to further reduce child labor by banning children under the age of 10 from coal mine work.

1846
The **Corn Laws** were eliminated. These laws had imposed high tariffs on imported grain to support domestic growers and lowered food prices. In reality, this gave factory owners an excuse to pay lower wages.

1847
The passage of the **Ten Hours Act** sought to prohibit textile factory owners from taking advantage of children (aged 13–18) and women by limiting the work shift to 10 hours per day.

Ask Yourself...

Which of the opposing forces, restoration or revolution, won out in the first half of the 19th century? Why do you think so?

1848 Revolutions 🔟

On January 12, 1848, there was a rebellion in the Kingdom of the Two Sicilies against King Ferdinand II. This rebellion was to be the first of approximately 50 revolts that convulsed Europe in the first four months of that year. The rebellions were disjointed with very little cooperation or coordination between nations. However, there were a few key themes that ran through most of these contemporaneous upheavals.

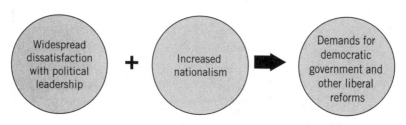

Widespread dissatisfaction with political leadership **+** Increased nationalism ➡ Demands for democratic government and other liberal reforms

---

 Did You Know?

💬 The 1840s were a terrible decade for agriculture and have accordingly been labeled the **"hungry forties."** The Irish experienced the most terrible conditions, with the Irish **potato famine** of 1845–1849 (1847 was the worst year) leading to the death of one million individuals and the emigration of an additional million out of Ireland.

1848 in France 🔟

There is an old saying that when France coughs, the rest of Europe catches a cold. In 1848, a rebellion in France blew up the powderkeg of revolutions that the rebellion in the Two Sicilies ignited. However, the 1848 movement is not a straightforward event that occurred due to a few simple causes. There are many factors that led to it and laid the groundwork for its outcome. Perhaps it is best to think of 1848 in France as a three-act film with a beginning, a middle, and an end.

**ACT I:
A Tale of Two Revolutions**

**ACT II:
June Days**

**ACT III:
Like Uncle, Like Nephew**

Setting:
Paris: July Monarchy

Cast:
- Louis Philippe
- François Guizot, chief minister
- Workers angry at the bourgeoisie-dominated July Monarchy

Plot Points:
- Workers secretly meet to plan liberal reforms.
- Guizot catches wind and bans the meetings.
- Louis Philippe placates the liberals by firing Guizot.
- Still dissatisified, the workers cause Louis Philippe to flee to England.
- Political disagreements between liberals and radical workers threaten the revolution.

Setting:
Paris: awaiting a new government

Cast:
- Louis Blanc, socialist writer

Plot Points:
- While liberals want political reform, radicals aim for economic change.
- Louis Blanc leads a group of radicals to create national workshops, which provide jobs.
- As a backlash to the radical changes, the April election sees a moderate assembly elected to run the provisional government.
- The assembly disbands the workshops.
- In response, radicals take to the streets in a class struggle known as "June Days," which saw 10,000 people killed.

Setting:
Paris: French Second Republic

Cast:
- Louis Napoleon, nephew of Napoleon Bonaparte

Plot Points:
- In November, moderate republicans create the Second Republic, to be headed by a president.
- Louis Napoleon campaigns on his name and empty platitudes to the working class.
- Louis Napoleon wins the presidency.
- During a constitutional crisis three years later, Louis Napoleon claims dictatorial powers.
- The following year, he declares himself Emperor Napoleon III.

1848 in the German States !

Recall that at this point, there is no unified Germany, but rather a series of states that all share a similar national identity known as "German." Let's look at the revolutionary movements in a few different states before tackling the larger issue of German unification.

A Prussian Revolution 💬

In Prussia, **Frederick William IV** (r. 1840–1861) had promised to promote moderate reform for many years, but he never implemented any changes.

March 1848: Protests erupt in Berlin, with two people killed by gun fire.	Horrified by the bloodshed, Frederick ordered his army to leave the city, which left him with no defense.	Frederick held an election to create an assembly tasked with designing a new Prussia constitution.	As time passed, the king was confident enough to call back the troops, and the constituent assembly was dissolved.	In December 1848, the king did draw up his own constitution, which was rather close to what the assembly had planned.

Frederick William IV's Constitution:

- Freedom of the Press
- Two-house legislature
- Adult-male universal suffrage for the lower house

In the end, adult-male universal suffrage was watered down by giving weighted votes to those who paid more taxes.

Nationalism Erupts in Austria 〰️

In Austria, news of the revolution in France inspired assorted nationalists to break free from the control of the Austrian monarchy.

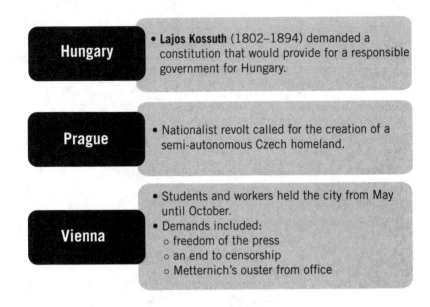

Hungary
- **Lajos Kossuth** (1802–1894) demanded a constitution that would provide for a responsible government for Hungary.

Prague
- Nationalist revolt called for the creation of a semi-autonomous Czech homeland.

Vienna
- Students and workers held the city from May until October.
- Demands included:
  - freedom of the press
  - an end to censorship
  - Metternich's ouster from office

Although Austrian **Emperor Ferdinand I**, not wanting bloodshed, initially called off troops, military force eventually put an end to each movement: his army put down the revolt in Prague by June, Vienna by November, and the Hungarian rebellion was finally squelched with help from Russia. By the end of the year, Ferdinand left the throne to his nephew Franz Joseph I, who reaffirmed absolutist rule in Austria.

A Unified Germany? 💿

Another notable event in 1848 was a concerted effort to establish a unified German state. On May 18, elected representatives from all the German states formed the **Frankfurt Parliament** to participate in what they thought was going to be the birth of a nation. The plan to unify Germany did not come into fruition at this point in history due to several competing points of view.

Type of Goverment

Disagreement: Participants could not agree whether the new Germany should be a monarchy or a republic.

Outcome: While all wanted to see a unified German nation, the Frankfurt Parliament could not come to a compromise on this issue.

Drawing up Borders

Disagreement: The **Grossdeutsch** plan called for all German lands, including parts of Austria and Bohemia, united under German rule.

Kleindeutsch supporters felt that the more realistic solution would be to include only Prussia and the smaller German States.

Outcome: The delegates chose Kleindeutsch and offered the German Imperial throne to Frederick William IV, the King of Prussia, who declined the offer, stating that he did not want a "crown picked up from the gutter."

This was a lost opportunity to build a German nation under a liberal parliament rather than by a militaristic Prussian state, as would be the case in 1871. Perhaps the future course of German history would have been very different had Germany united under a liberal parliament.

1848 in the Italian States 💬

The individual states in Italy all had varying degrees of success in their revolutions.

Location of Revolution	Immediate Response by State	Outcome of Revolution
Sicily	Liberal charter granted	The king's power was restored, and the charter ended.
Tuscany	Liberal charter granted	After fleeing, Grand Duke Leopold II returned with the help of Austrians and rescinded the charter.
Sardinia	Liberal charter granted	Charter was sustained up until Italian unification (1871).
Papal States	Liberal charter granted	The Roman Republic lasted for several months, though the pope was reinstalled with help from the French. As the French themselves were largely liberal, the revived papal states included liberal reforms.
Lombardy-Venetia (northern Italian kingdom dominated by Austria)	The revolution led to a call by Italian liberals for a war of unification. **Charles Albert**, the ruler of the Kingdom of Sardinia, reluctantly took up the banner of Italian nationalists.	Italian nationalists were easily defeated by the Austrians.

Lessons to Be Learned 😬

Liberals in Italy who wanted a unified nation could take a few lessons from the experiences of 1848:

Three Lessons Learned from Italy's 1848 Revolutions

- A unified Italy would not grow out of the papacy.
- The Kingdom of Sardinia could serve as the foundation for a unified state since, out of the group of Italian states that were granted constitutions in 1848, only Sardinia governed via the constitutional monarchy in the following years.
- The Italians could not eject Austria from its possessions within Italy without the aid of another European power.

Remember these lessons in just a few pages!

😬 Following the revolutions of 1848, the Austrian Empire, now under the rule of **Emperor Francis Joseph** (r. 1848–1916), relied heavily on military force to subdue all forms of liberalism and nationalism. Magyars, Slavs, Italians, and Germans would have to wait to see nationalist reforms realized.

Russia and Great Britain: Outliers Once Again ❗

Perhaps not surprisingly, two nations avoided the turmoil of revolution in 1848: Russia and Great Britain.

Repression in Russia was so complete under the reign of Nicholas I that 1848 passed with hardly a yawn.

Russia

The British saw a peaceful establishment of liberal reforms* due to a movement known as **Chartism**, which centered on the belief that the problems of the working class could be corrected by changes in the political organization of the country.

Great Britain

The **People's Charter of 1838**, from which the movement received its name, contained six points:

- universal adult-male suffrage (some Chartists did favor female suffrage as well)
- the secret ballot
- abolition of property requirements for Members of Parliament
- payment to Members of Parliament
- equal electoral districts
- annual parliaments with yearly elections

---

*Britain's reform was incremental: by the beginning of the 20th century, five of the six acts of the Charter were established parts of the British Constitution. Only the annual parliaments did not pass.

Did You Know?

💬 Nicholas's successor, **Alexander II,** oversaw Russia's first significant liberal reform—the Emancipation Reform of 1861, which served to abolish the institution of serfdom, a system of manorial bondage dating back to the Middle Ages.

1848 Scorecard ❗

So what was the outcome after a year of revolutions?

More Liberal	Unchanged	More Repressive
Prussia	Austrian Empire	France
Sardinia	Tuscany	Sicily
Great Britain	Lombardy-Venetia	Russia

Ask Yourself...

- What social and political trends contributed to the movements of 1848?
- To what extent was the British Chartism approach more or less successful than the uprisings throughout Europe in 1848?

Industrial Revolution ❗

The **Industrial Revolution** was a period that saw the development of factories, bringing an end to the **domestic system** of production that had guided manufacturing since the early modern period. While this transition had been ongoing for centuries, the second half of the 18th century saw a quickening of the process. By the middle of the 19th century, particularly with the advent of the railroad, industrialization was beginning to reshape the European landscape and to dramatically alter the way in which people lived.

Great Britain at the Forefront ❗

Great Britain was the first European nation to begin the process of industrialization. Let's look at the possible reasons that contributed to this:

Agricultural Revolution
- 18th-century scientific farming techniques allowed for an increase in crop yield.
- Population almost doubled over the course of the 18th century, due in large part to a lower death rate, thanks to better diet and hygiene; this created a large low-wage work force.
- England began to dabble in **manufacturing industries**.
- The **Enclosure Acts** forced small-scale farmers into urban areas, increasing the efficiency of the now-larger farms and providing a low-paid workforce for the factories.

Overseas trade
- The 18th century witnessed a significant increase in Great Britain's overseas trade.
- Supplied additional investment capital.
- Provided the nation with the world's largest merchant marine.
- The 18th century saw the height of the Atlantic slave trade.

Geography
- Transportation in Great Britain was enhanced by the fact that the entire nation lies within close proximity to the sea.
- Canals made water transport efficient.
- Great Britain contained the two critical natural resources of the Early Industrial Revolution: **coal** and **iron**.

Liberalism
- Great Britain's **political stability** created an environment friendly to economic investment.
- Religious minorities faced no barriers to economic participation thanks to **religious toleration** in Great Britain.

Major Industrial Breakthroughs 🔊

Here are some of the key inventions that helped move the Industrial Revolution along:

Invention	Inventor	Year	Purpose
Smelt Iron	Abraham Darby	1709	Efficiently produced iron
Flying shuttle	John Kay	1733	Increased the speed at which weavers could make cloth
Spinning Jenny	James Hargreaves	1764	Could spin multiple threads at once as to not outstrip the supply of thread
Water frame	Richard Arkwright	1767	Combined spindles and rollers to create a spinning machine to spin cloth
Steam engine	James Watt	1776	By pushing steam into each end of a closed cylinder, resulting in the upward and downward movement of the pistons, the engine made factories independent of waterpower and increased the pace of industry.

Note that these labor-saving devices were in the field of cloth production. Labor-saving was useful because British cloth manufacturing was constrained by labor supply: thanks to cotton imports (from colonization of India and trade with the American South) and increased wool supply (due to enclosure and the agricultural revolution), labor savings actually resulted in more cloth to sell, giving factory cloth producers a strong price advantage over their competition. However, the cotton industry came at a cost: the cotton imports that fueled the Industrial Revolution were available only because of colonization and slavery.

The Railroad 💬

Iron and steam were the combination behind perhaps the most important invention of the 19th-century Industrial Revolution—the **railroad**.

1830 Britain: The rail network

The first exclusively steam-powered passenger railroad traveled between Liverpool and Manchester in 1830.

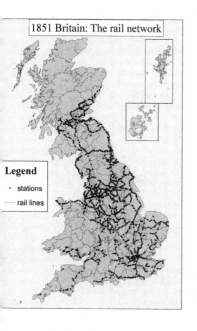

1851 Britain: The rail network

Legend
· stations
— rail lines

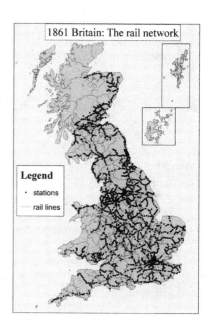

1861 Britain: The rail network

Legend
· stations
— rail lines

By the middle of the century, railroad tracks crisscrossed Britain, transporting both passengers and goods.

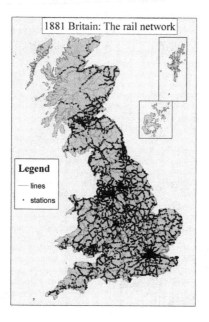

1881 Britain: The rail network

Legend
— lines
· stations

The railroads had an immense impact on the economy. It is estimated that by 1880, one in ten jobs in Great Britain was in some way connected either directly with the railroads or with services tied to rail transportation.

Belgium and Prussia Adopt British Methods

The British took the lead in manufacturing, but it wasn't long before methods pioneered by the British appeared on the continent. Belgium was the first to industrialize, possibly because, like Great Britain, it had a plentiful supply of coal and iron. Other nations industrialized with varying degrees of rapidity.

The German states were hampered by numerous tolls and tariffs, making the transportation of goods extremely expensive. To aid in the spread of trade and manufacturing, Prussia took the lead in 1834 by creating the *Zollverein*, a customs union that abolished tariffs between the German states.

What About France?

As certain German states, most notably Prussia, achieved significant industrial growth by the middle of the 19th century, France lagged behind by comparison. Looking at how France compared to Great Britain during the early part of the Industrial Revolution may shine some light on why this was so:

- Enjoyed a stable political system
- Maintained centralized banking
- Experienced rapid population growth
- Peasants had little choice but to go to the cities in search of low-paying factory jobs.

Great Britain

- Political instability in the first half of the 19th century
- Lacked centralized banking
- Population growth only half that of other European nations
- Peasants remained relatively content to stay on the land.

France

Did You Know?

 French Contributions to Industrialization

In certain industries, such as the manufacturing of luxury goods, the French took the lead, and while their economic growth was not quite as dramatic as the growth of the British and Prussian models, it remained constant throughout most of the 19th century.

German economist Friedrich List saw national economics not as the invisible hand that Adam Smith envisioned, but rather as a carefully directed process aimed at improving a nation's standing in the world. List advocated a **national system** that included imposing tariffs to keep foreign goods out of German lands, as well as using national funds for practical enterprises (infrastructure, such as railroads). Pay attention in the coming sections to how List's ideas influenced how Germany took control of its own development, starting with Otto von Bismarck.

Impact of Industrialization ❗

Industrialization dramatically changed life in Europe. Because the location of factories tended to be concentrated in certain areas, cities began to grow and develop rapidly. The change from rural manufacturing to bringing workers to a location significantly affected life in Britain.

Dirty Old Town 🔴

Unfortunately, the cities that grew from the ground up as a result of industrialization tended to be awful places for the working poor. Mortality rates were significantly higher for urban dwellers than for those who resided in the countryside.

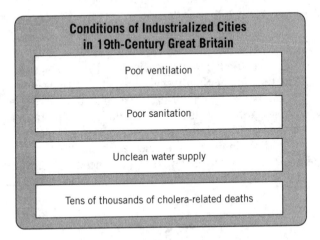

Conditions of Industrialized Cities in 19th-Century Great Britain

Poor ventilation

Poor sanitation

Unclean water supply

Tens of thousands of cholera-related deaths

Did You Know?

💬 By the middle of the 19th century, Great Britain became the first nation to have more people living in the cities than in the countryside, one of the most dramatic transformations in the history of humankind.

Child Labor 🔴

Industrialization greatly affected the family structure. The fact that the entire family was working was not new; the earlier domestic system had relied on the family as a cohesive working unit. What was different was that the family no longer worked together under one roof.

Women and children worked under conditions even more deplorable than the men did.

Great Britain's Sadler Committee exposed that children were being beaten in the factories.

As a result, the House of Commons passed the **Factory Act of 1833.**

Factory Act
- Children younger than nine could not work in textile mills.
- Children younger than 12 could work no more than nine hours per day.
- Children younger than 18 couldn't work more than twelve hours each day.

Working-Class Responses to Industrialization ❗

At first, workers were befuddled as to how to grapple with the economic and social problems caused by industrialization.

Luddites
- Some laborers tried to destroy the machines.
  - Their fictional leader was Ned Ludd.
    - The term "Luddite" has stayed in the modern vocabulary in reference to those who refuse to embrace new technologies.

Textile workers
- Handloom weavers and other workers viewed their traditional way of life as threatened by machinery.

Farmers
- Machinery also caused hardship for many laborers on the farms.
  - They created an imaginary character known as "Captain Swing," who righted the wrongs imposed on hardworking individuals by the advent of technology.

Cooperative Societies 💬

After these rather primitive means of dealing with industrialization proved to be ineffective, workers sought to create **cooperative societies**, small associations within a given trade that provided funeral benefits and other services for their members.

Evolution of Unions 💬

Unions were a critical reason for the steady improvement in wages and factory conditions that took place in the second half of the 19th century.

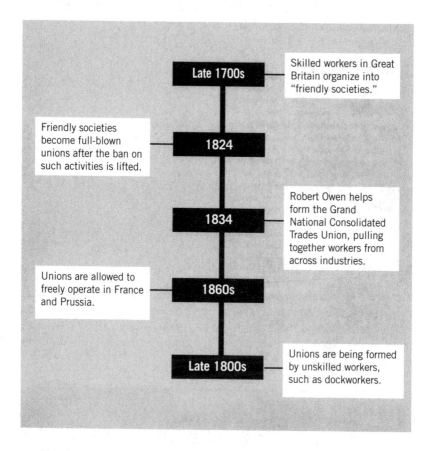

Late 1700s — Skilled workers in Great Britain organize into "friendly societies."

Friendly societies become full-blown unions after the ban on such activities is lifted. — **1824**

1834 — Robert Owen helps form the Grand National Consolidated Trades Union, pulling together workers from across industries.

Unions are allowed to freely operate in France and Prussia. — **1860s**

Late 1800s — Unions are being formed by unskilled workers, such as dockworkers.

Socialism and Karl Marx ❶

Some workers—particularly on the continent—found that although the unions' emphasis on gradual improvements in wages and hours worked, it was at best only a partial solution to the problems caused by industrialization. Many turned to **socialism**, believing that it offered a complete overhaul to an oppressive society.

Karl Marx
1818–1883

- Met his colleague **Friedrich Engels** (1820–1895) in England
- Along with Engels, organized a **Communist League** to link the far-flung German Socialists, many of whom, like Marx, were living in exile

A Theory of History ❶

Marx and Engels believed that all history, from the beginnings of time, consists of the struggle between social classes, an idea that was labeled as historical materialism, or the material dialectic. In essence, Marx makes a prediction about how the classes will clash some time in the future (at the end of capitalism):

Marx's Predictions About the Future

- The proletariat will arise and supplant those capitalists who had exploited them.
- Initially, the state will dominate in a violent, though triumphant, struggle by the workers.
- Eventually, the state withers away when it is no longer needed as a result of the elimination of all other classes besides the proletariat.

The feudal age was supplanted by the triumph of the bourgeois class in the 19th century.

The development of capitalism led to the creation of a new class, the **proletariat** (the working class).

In this respect, the term **Marxism** refers to a theory about history.

Marx's Book Club 💬

Karl Marx is closely associated with two texts:

Communist Manifesto (1848)	Das Kapital (1867)
Marx and Engels teamed up to write this pamphlet, which served as a basic statement of principles for the Communist League.	An enormous treatise on capitalism, which explains the mechanics by which capitalists extract profit from labor.

Marx Goes International 💬

Marx brought a revolutionary dynamism to the class struggle, because he believed that the working class had to constantly prepare itself by organizing socialist parties. Two international communist organizations aimed at uniting the like-minded parties from around the world popped up in the 19th century:

First International	Second International
• Begun in 1864 • Not a completely Marxist organization—Trade Unionists, Mazzini Republicans, Marxists, and Anarchists were all members. • Folded in 1876 over internal conflicts	• Begun on July 14*, 1889 • Loose federation of the world's socialist parties heavily influenced by Marxism • Created by Engels after Marx's death

💬 The statement of General Rules for the International Workingmen's Association's [First International's], to which Marx contributed, states that the purpose was to "afford a central medium of communication and cooperation" for those organizations whose aim was the "protection, advancement, and complete emancipation of the working classes."

Ask Yourself...

To what extent did the Industrial Revolution improve conditions in Europe? To what extent did it hinder conditions?

---

*It was, of course, no accident that the first meeting of the Second International took place on the hundredth anniversary of the storming of the Bastille—Marxists were consciously referencing the beginning of the French Revolution and calling for one of their own.

The Age of National Unification (1854–1871) 🛑

By the early 19th century, individuals in both the German and Italian states sought to create a nation-state that would unite all Italians or all Germans under one political banner because they shared either a common culture, or language, or a fear of foreign domination. This process of national unification would have a tremendous impact on the future course of European history.

The Crimean War (1853–1856) 💬

This conflict was the first European war since the Napoleonic era. The main issue was the fear among British and French statesmen that Ottoman weakness was encouraging Russian adventurism in the Balkans and the possibility that the Russians might gain access to the Mediterranean by occupying the port city of Istanbul.

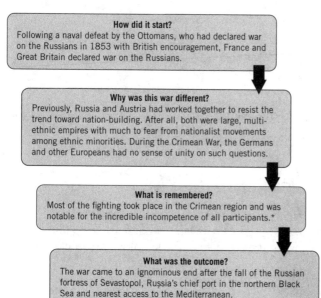

How did it start?
Following a naval defeat by the Ottomans, who had declared war on the Russians in 1853 with British encouragement, France and Great Britain declared war on the Russians.

Why was this war different?
Previously, Russia and Austria had worked together to resist the trend toward nation-building. After all, both were large, multi-ethnic empires with much to fear from nationalist movements among ethnic minorities. During the Crimean War, the Germans and other Europeans had no sense of unity on such questions.

What is remembered?
Most of the fighting took place in the Crimean region and was notable for the incredible incompetence of all participants.*

What was the outcome?
The war came to an ignominious end after the fall of the Russian fortress of Sevastopol, Russia's chief port in the northern Black Sea and nearest access to the Mediterranean.

---

*Most of the half-million casualties did not die in battle but perished due to disease in filthy field hospitals, something that inspired **Florence Nightingale** (1820–1910) to revolutionize the nursing profession.

Why Does the Crimean War Matter? 💬

Three reasons:

1. This was a major blow to Russian ambitions of involvement in European politics.
2. The **Concert of Europe**, the idea that the great powers (France, Prussia, Austria, Russia, and Great Britain) should work together—a concept that emerged from the Congress of Vienna—was finally shattered.
3. The British public was horrified by the course of events in the Crimean region; as a result, Great Britain became more isolationist regarding European affairs.

Impact on Nation Building ❗

When Austria stood in opposition to the building of states in Germany and Italy, it received no support from an embittered Russia, and when France found itself confronting Prussia in 1870, it would find little sympathy from the British.

 Did You Know?

 Alfred Lord Tennyson's famous poem, "The Charge of the Light Brigade," captures battlefield stupidity during the Crimean War.

The Unification of Italy ❗

In 1848, Italian liberals made an aborted attempt to create an Italian state. Although the attempt failed, the dream for a state never disappeared. Following the collapse of the short-lived Roman Republic, **Pope Pius IX**—when his authority in Rome was restored—inspired increasingly reactionary policies. Liberals no longer saw any potential for the realization of a federation of Italian states headed by the pope.

Recall that what we now refer to as Italy was a series of kingdoms on the peninsula:

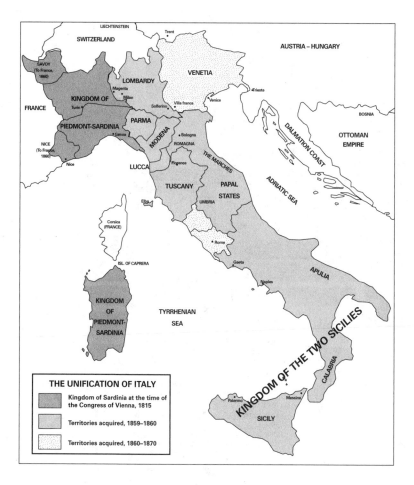

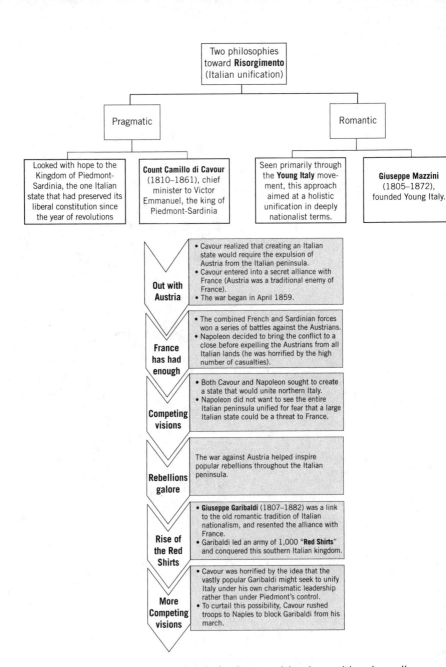

Two philosophies toward **Risorgimento** (Italian unification)

Pragmatic

Looked with hope to the Kingdom of Piedmont-Sardinia, the one Italian state that had preserved its liberal constitution since the year of revolutions

Count Camillo di Cavour (1810–1861), chief minister to Victor Emmanuel, the king of Piedmont-Sardinia

Romantic

Seen primarily through the **Young Italy** movement, this approach aimed at a holistic unification in deeply nationalist terms.

Giuseppe Mazzini (1805–1872), founded Young Italy.

Out with Austria
- Cavour realized that creating an Italian state would require the expulsion of Austria from the Italian peninsula.
- Cavour entered into a secret alliance with France (Austria was a traditional enemy of France).
- The war began in April 1859.

France has had enough
- The combined French and Sardinian forces won a series of battles against the Austrians.
- Napoleon decided to bring the conflict to a close before expelling the Austrians from all Italian lands (he was horrified by the high number of casualties).

Competing visions
- Both Cavour and Napoleon sought to create a state that would unite northern Italy.
- Napoleon did not want to see the entire Italian peninsula unified for fear that a large Italian state could be a threat to France.

Rebellions galore

The war against Austria helped inspire popular rebellions throughout the Italian peninsula.

Rise of the Red Shirts
- **Giuseppe Garibaldi** (1807–1882) was a link to the old romantic tradition of Italian nationalism, and resented the alliance with France.
- Garibaldi led an army of 1,000 **"Red Shirts"** and conquered this southern Italian kingdom.

More Competing visions
- Cavour was horrified by the idea that the vastly popular Garibaldi might seek to unify Italy under his own charismatic leadership rather than under Piedmont's control.
- To curtail this possibility, Cavour rushed troops to Naples to block Garibaldi from his march.

Cavour was actually interested only in the papal lands, and he shrewdly waited for a popular revolt in the papal states to commence. Only then, under the pretext of restoring order, did he move Sardinian troops into all of the lands controlled by the pope except for the city of Rome.

ASAP European History

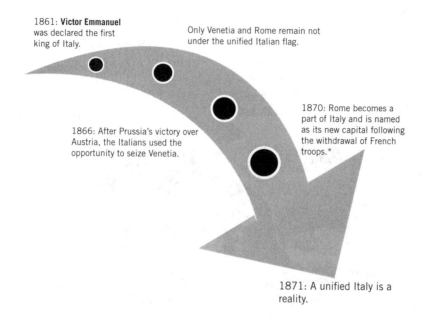

1861: **Victor Emmanuel** was declared the first king of Italy.

Only Venetia and Rome remain not under the unified Italian flag.

1866: After Prussia's victory over Austria, the Italians used the opportunity to seize Venetia.

1870: Rome becomes a part of Italy and is named as its new capital following the withdrawal of French troops.*

1871: A unified Italy is a reality.

The Unification of Germany 🛑

Although Italian unification had important implications for the rest of Europe, the rise of a unified German state in 1871 totally altered the balance of power in Europe, owing to the great military and economic strength of this new state.

There were two important factors at play in this process. They both tie back to the Napoleonic Wars:

1. Napoleon's domination of large parts of Germany increased the demand among German patriots for the creation of a unified nation.
2. Napoleon's conquests reduced the number of independent German states, which simplified the actual process of unification.

---

*The French withdrawal from Rome was due to France's obligations in the **Franco-Prussian War**. More about that soon!

Why Prussia? ❶

Following the fall of Napoleon, Austria and Prussia were the two dominant states within the German Confederation. Although it was not a foregone conclusion that it was to be Prussia rather than Austria that would take the lead in creating a unified Germany, Prussia did enjoy a number of significant advantages.

Reasons for Prussia's Leadership Among the German States

- ☑ Prussia, through its creation of the *Zollverein*, had achieved an economic preeminence over the other member states.
- ☑ Prussia had achieved a significant measure of industrialization, while Austria remained a primarily agricultural state.
- ☑ Austria was specifically excluded by Prussia for membership in the *Zollverein* customs union.
- ☑ The Austrian Empire was a polyglot state made up of numerous nationalities, while Prussia was primarily a German state.
- ☑ Most important to its dominance, Prussia enjoyed the services of **Otto von Bismarck** (1815–1898).

Blood and Iron

On taking the throne of Prussia, **William I** (r. 1861–1888) made the most important decision of his reign when he selected Bismarck as his prime minister. Bismarck, a Junker (Prussian noble), was known for his arch-conservative views. Standing before the parliamentary budget commission, Bismarck delivered his **"Blood and Iron"** speech:

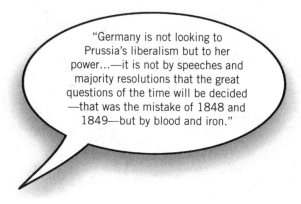

"Germany is not looking to Prussia's liberalism but to her power...—it is not by speeches and majority resolutions that the great questions of the time will be decided —that was the mistake of 1848 and 1849—but by blood and iron."

Otto von Bismarck's War Games

Bismarck rose to power (and remained in power for over 25 years) thanks to his careful manipulation of the press and the monarchs of Germany. The key to his plan to create a unified German state was to modernize the Prussian army by giving it the latest weapons. The first stage in this plan took place in 1864 and involved an alliance with Austria against Denmark over the disputed territories of Schleswig and Holstein.

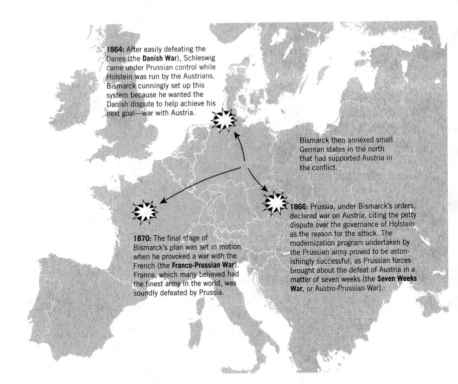

1864: After easily defeating the Danes (the **Danish War**), Schleswig came under Prussian control while Holstein was run by the Austrians. Bismarck cunningly set up this system because he wanted the Danish dispute to help achieve his next goal—war with Austria.

Bismarck then annexed small German states in the north that had supported Austria in the conflict.

1866: Prussia, under Bismarck's orders, declared war on Austria, citing the petty dispute over the governance of Holstein as the reason for the attack. The modernization program undertaken by the Prussian army proved to be astonishingly successful, as Prussian forces brought about the defeat of Austria in a matter of seven weeks (the **Seven Weeks War**, or Austro-Prussian War).

1870: The final stage of Bismarck's plan was set in motion when he provoked a war with the French (the **Franco-Prussian War**). France, which many believed had the finest army in the world, was soundly defeated by Prussia.

Using Prussia's newfound prestige earned by achieving this victory, Bismarck was able to either convince or bribe the rulers of the other German states to accept the creation of a Germany under Prussian leadership. On January 18, 1871, William I was proclaimed in the palace of Versailles as German emperor. Bismarck, on the other hand, was forced into early retirement in 1890.

The creation of a German Empire completely changed the direction of European history. The following are some examples:

- The new German state created a bitter enemy of France, which lost the territories of Alsace and Lorraine and was forced to pay a huge indemnity to Germany for having started the war.
- The economic power of this new German state created rising tensions with Great Britain and helped set into motion the rush to build colonial empires in the last quarter of the 19th century. The mad scramble began when Bismarck encouraged the French to build an empire in Africa to distract from the loss of Alsace-Lorraine.
- Eventually, all the nations of Europe sought to create overseas empires as a means to further their political and economic interests within a Europe that was trying to adjust to the tensions that arose from the development of a powerful German state.

Kulturkampf 💬

Prior to being put out to pasture, Bismarck had worried about the internal dangers facing the new nation and therefore attacked two groups he deemed to be a threat to the internal cohesion of the Reich—the Catholics and the Socialists.

	Catholics	Socialists
Bismarck's concern	Catholic Germans may place their loyalty to the Church above that of German nationalism.	Socialists valued empowering the proletariat above nationalist goals.
Bismarck's action	**Kulturkampf**—a policy in which church appointments and oversight of Catholic education fell under the purview of Bismarck	Called for the passage in the Reichstag of a ban on Socialists' right to assemble, as well as attempted to limit the political appeal of the Socialists by establishing old-age pensions and other social benefits for all Germans

After Bismarck 💬

Prussia (and later, Germany) was a conservative, aristocratic state. Bismarck ruled at the pleasure of the king, not the people; his poor relations with Wilhelm II led to less able statesmen taking his place, jeopardizing his fragile peace with Russia, and ultimately sacrificing German stability for the sake of German glory.

The 19th Century Elsewhere in Europe ❗

France's Second Empire and Third Republic ❗

France seemed to have a tortured existence throughout the 19th century as it continued to grapple with the legacy of the French Revolution. However, France prospered greatly during the first 10 years of the reign of **Napoleon III**. Cheap credit provided by the government allowed for a significant economic expansion during this period.

Georges-Eugène, commonly known as Baron Haussmann (1809–1891), was appointed by Napoleon III to modernize Paris. Notably, he...

...cleared many of the slums of the city and in their place built the wide avenues that we think of when we imagine Paris.

...utilized aqueducts to bring fresh water into the city and sewers to remove waste, resulting in the elimination of one of the great scourges of the earlier part of the century—cholera.

Despite the economic improvements during the first decade of his reign, Napoleon III led a politically authoritarian regime. Beginning in 1860, Napoleon began to make a number of concessions, such as lifting censorship laws and declaring France a "**liberal empire**." However, these reforms would not sustain his empire.

France's Terrible Horrible No-Good Very Bad Year: 1870

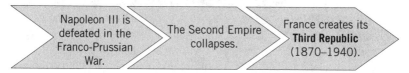

Napoleon III is defeated in the Franco-Prussian War. > The Second Empire collapses. > France creates its **Third Republic** (1870–1940).

Right away, the Republic had to deal with the daunting task of putting down a revolt in Paris, which resulted in the rise of the **Paris Commune**, a radical government created out of the anarchy brought about by the Franco-Prussian War. The republican government restored order in Paris only after winning an armed struggle that resulted in the massacre of 25,000 Parisians. By 1875, the republic was firmly established:

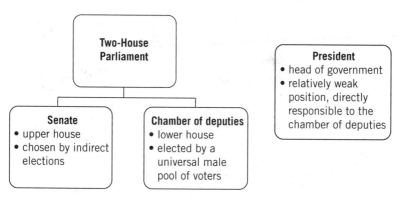

Two-House Parliament

Senate
• upper house
• chosen by indirect elections

Chamber of deputies
• lower house
• elected by a universal male pool of voters

President
• head of government
• relatively weak position, directly responsible to the chamber of deputies

The Third Republic faced its greatest challenge in 1889, when a *coup d' état* looked probable. A wildly popular general named Georges Boulanger reformed the military, used troops to put down labor strikes, and manipulated the press to paint him as a patriot to such an extent that he secured the support of the military, business leaders, and even the rural poor. After being elected president, Boulanger tried to take his power one step further by presenting a referendum that would declare him French dictator. The initiative ultimately did not pass and the Third Republic survived the **Boulanger Affair** to live another day.

Victorian England 💬

In contrast to France, Great Britain enjoyed remarkable stability and prosperity in the second half of the 19th century. A general sense of self-satisfaction pervaded Victorian England:

National Pride	Liberal Reforms
The Great Exhibition of 1851* boasted more than 13,000 exhibitors displaying the variety of British goods that were now available as a result of industrialization.	In 1867, the **Second Reform Act** passed, which extended the vote to urban heads of households, and in 1884, the vote was further extended to heads of households in the countryside.

Under **Queen Victoria** (r. 1837–1901), Great Britain's political game shifted toward a more independent parliament, resulting in less influence from the monarchy. Equally notable from this period was the development of British politics as a rivalry between two ruling parties.

Tory

- Conservative party
- **Benjamin Disraeli** led the party as prime minister during part of Queen Victoria's reign.

Liberal

- Closely associated with labor
- **William Gladstone,** a fierce rival of Disraeli, once represented the party as British prime minister.

---

*An observer of the Great Exhibition noted that the **Crystal Palace**, a prefabricated building that hosted the exhibits and the millions of visitors, was "the aesthetic bloom of its practical character, and of the practical tendency of the English nation."

Russian Reforms? 💬

The stresses of war can show a nation at its best or they can reveal significant problems. For Russia, the poor showing in the Crimean War, fought in its own backyard, revealed the backwardness of its society in comparison to the nations of western Europe. Although Nicholas I was far too reactionary to contemplate reform, his successor, **Alexander II**, attempted some reforms, tentative though they may have been:

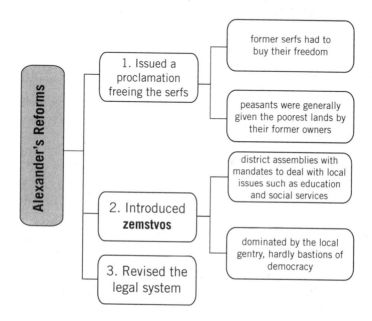

Alexander's Reforms

1. Issued a proclamation freeing the serfs
- former serfs had to buy their freedom
- peasants were generally given the poorest lands by their former owners

2. Introduced **zemstvos**
- district assemblies with mandates to deal with local issues such as education and social services
- dominated by the local gentry, hardly bastions of democracy

3. Revised the legal system

Despite these "reforms," Alexander remained an autocrat and saw no need to implement fundamental changes like the introduction of a written constitution and parliamentary bodies.

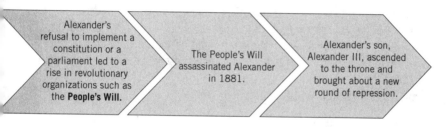

Alexander's refusal to implement a constitution or a parliament led to a rise in revolutionary organizations such as the **People's Will**.

The People's Will assassinated Alexander in 1881.

Alexander's son, Alexander III, ascended to the throne and brought about a new round of repression.

The Struggles of Austria

The 19th century was essentially a decades-long "rough day at the office" for the Austrian Empire, a multinational empire in an age of growing nationalist sentiment.

Some Lowlights from the Late 19th Century in Austria

- ☑ By 1866, Austria had lost all of its territories in Italy.
- ☑ It experienced a shattering defeat by the Prussians at the Battle of Sadowa.
- ☑ Austria was no longer viewed as a factor in German affairs.
- ☑ In 1867, the government in Vienna signed an agreement with the Magyars in Hungary, creating a dual Austro-Hungarian empire.

 Did You Know?

Austria and Hungary were each independent but united under the mutual leadership of **Francis Joseph,** who became Emperor of Austria and King of Hungary.

Perhaps not surprisingly, the Magyars, having achieved a measure of independence, turned around and did their best to ensure that the Croats, Serbs, Romanians, and other nationalities located within Hungary were denied any form of self-rule. As a result of a lessening influence in western Europe, Austria-Hungary attempted to become more influential in the Balkan region. What could go wrong?

The Sick Man Attempts Modernization 💬

Another multinational empire at the crossroads was the Ottoman Empire. Commonly referred to as "the sick man of Europe," the Ottoman state attempted in the second half of the 19th century to implement a process of modernization.

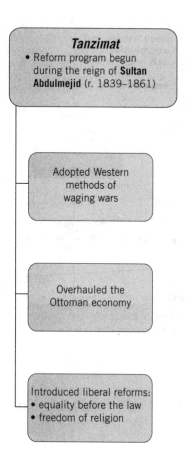

Tanzimat
- Reform program begun during the reign of **Sultan Abdulmejid** (r. 1839–1861)

Adopted Western methods of waging wars

Overhauled the Ottoman economy

Introduced liberal reforms:
- equality before the law
- freedom of religion

The introduction of Western education played a significant role in forming a group of liberal intellectuals known as the **"Young Turks."**

The Young Turks pushed reform further than the government had ever planned and, in 1876, helped establish the Ottoman state as a constitutional monarchy.

The brutal Sultan Abdul Hamid II (r. 1876–1909) scrapped the constitution as part of his attempt to subjugate the non-Muslim peoples within his empire.

The Ottomans could do little but sit idly by when, at the **Congress of Berlin** (1878), after another humiliating defeat at the hands of the Russians (the **Russo-Turkish War**), the other European powers recognized the independence of Serbia, Montenegro, Romania, and Bulgaria—all former Ottoman territories in the same Balkan region where the Austro-Hungarian Empire would soon have so much trouble.

Ask Yourself...

- Why might unification have been inevitable in Germany and Italy?
- To what extent were the factors that led to unifications in Germany and Italy present in other parts of Europe during this time period?

The Second Industrial
Revolution

By the middle of the 19th century, Europe had undergone a dramatic process of economic expansion. These economic changes—sometimes referred to as the Second Industrial Revolution—and their impact on human lives were even greater than what occurred during the initial stages of industrialization.

Did You Know?

❷ Because of its strength and durability, steel became the metal of choice for building and ships, resulting in a revolution in architecture and shipbuilding.

Steel
The label "Age of Steel" is an apt one for the second half of the 19th century.

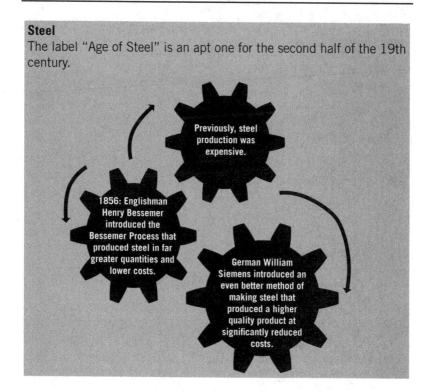

Previously, steel production was expensive.

1856: Englishman Henry Bessemer introduced the Bessemer Process that produced steel in far greater quantities and lower costs.

German William Siemens introduced an even better method of making steel that produced a higher quality product at significantly reduced costs.

Electricity

Few developments have affected the way people live their lives as significantly as the invention of the means to harness electrical power.

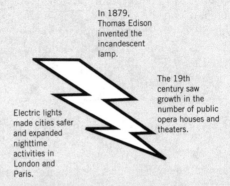

In 1879, Thomas Edison invented the incandescent lamp.

The 19th century saw growth in the number of public opera houses and theaters.

Electric lights made cities safer and expanded nighttime activities in London and Paris.

Transportation

The second half of the 19th century witnessed many significant developments in all forms of transportation.

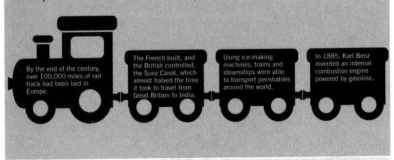

By the end of the century, over 100,000 miles of rail track had been laid in Europe.

The French built, and the British controlled, the Suez Canal, which almost halved the time it took to travel from Great Britain to India.

Using ice-making machines, trains and steamships were able to transport perishables around the world.

In 1885, Karl Benz invented an internal combustion engine powered by gasoline.

Communication

Britain was the first European nation to establish a national postal system.

The development of universal public education also meant that more people were inclined to communicate in writing.

The first telegraph line was completed in 1844.

In 1876, Alexander Graham Bell invented the telephone.

Other Scientific Developments 🔊

Science began to play an increasingly important role in industrial expansion. In particular, the second half of the 19th century produced a series of major developments.

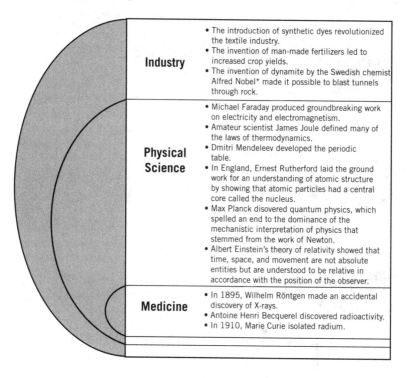

Industry	• The introduction of synthetic dyes revolutionized the textile industry. • The invention of man-made fertilizers led to increased crop yields. • The invention of dynamite by the Swedish chemist Alfred Nobel* made it possible to blast tunnels through rock.
Physical Science	• Michael Faraday produced groundbreaking work on electricity and electromagnetism. • Amateur scientist James Joule defined many of the laws of thermodynamics. • Dmitri Mendeleev developed the periodic table. • In England, Ernest Rutherford laid the ground work for an understanding of atomic structure by showing that atomic particles had a central core called the nucleus. • Max Planck disovered quantum physics, which spelled an end to the dominance of the mechanistic interpretation of physics that stemmed from the work of Newton. • Albert Einstein's theory of relativity showed that time, space, and movement are not absolute entities but are understood to be relative in accordance with the position of the observer.
Medicine	• In 1895, Wilhelm Röntgen made an accidental discovery of X-rays. • Antoine Henri Becquerel discovered radioactivity. • In 1910, Marie Curie isolated radium.

---

*Alfred Nobel was horrified by the potentially destructive uses of his invention, and in his will he entrusted money for a prize to be given in his name to those who served the cause of peace.

Philosophy 😐

Just as scientific inquiry was revealing ideas and principles that appeared to be less than rational, philosophers began to question and even to reject the ideas of the 18th-century Enlightenment.

Friedrich Nietzsche
- German philosopher
- Most influential work, *Thus Spake Zarathustra,* argued it was necessary to break free from traditional morality, and famously proclaimed "God is dead"
- Hated the Germany created by Bismarck and instead yearned for the emergence of the artist-warrior superman

Henri Bergson
- French philosopher
- Advocate of continental philosophy, a broad term that characterizes many European philosophers of the time who focused on the importance of immediacy and experience rather than on analytical thought

Georges Sorel
- French philosopher
- Saw human endeavors, as well as systems of thought (Marxism, for instance) as products of a human vulnerability toward myth (as opposed to "reality")
- Science, which he did not see as synonomous with nature, was one such myth

Psychoanalysis 😐

Sigmund Freud*
1856–1939

- Austrian psychologist and neurologist
- Father of psychoanalysis
- Took the methods of modern science and proposed to find a way to treat mental disorders by delving into the human subconscious
- Believed that dreams revealed the inner workings of a subconscious world

---

*In *Civilization and Its Discontents,* a book written in his more pessimistic later years, Freud questioned the very premise of continuous progress for the human race and instead posited that despite attempts to suppress it, violence lies at the very core of our being.

Medicine 💬

The beginnings of modern Western medicine took root in the 19th century, marking the first time in history that going to the doctor was not such a bad idea.

- Surgery, previously dominated by practitioners who bragged about their ability to remove a leg in under 90 seconds, was transformed in 1846 when American dentist **William Morton** began to introduce anesthesia in the form of ether, followed by the use of chloroform anesthesia a few years later.
- Overall, the most significant change in medicine in the period was that the experimental method found in the sciences was applied to medicine. Applying the experimental method, **Louis Pasteur** discovered that microbes—small, invisible organisms—caused diseases.
- Pasteur also explained how vaccines, which had been in use since the 18th century to fight against smallpox, worked within the body by stimulating the immune system to produce antibodies after coming into contact with a weak form of the bacilli.
- The English surgeon **Joseph Lister,** building on Pasteur's discoveries, initiated the use of carbolic acid as a disinfectant during surgery.
- A Hungarian doctor, **Ignaz Semmelweis,** made childbirth much safer for women, demonstrating that if doctors and nurses thoroughly washed their hands prior to delivery, it could dramatically reduce the number of women who died from what was known as "childbed fever."

Darwin 💬

Few individuals had a greater impact on the intellectual world of the 19th century than **Charles Darwin** (1809–1882), an English naturalist who traveled on the *H.M.S. Beagle* to the Galapagos Islands off the coast of South America.

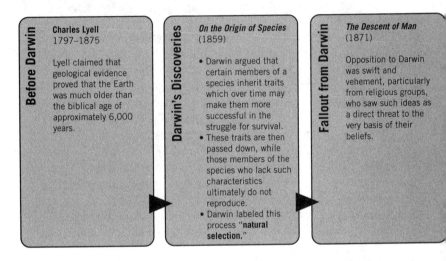

Before Darwin

Charles Lyell
1797–1875

Lyell claimed that geological evidence proved that the Earth was much older than the biblical age of approximately 6,000 years.

Darwin's Discoveries

On the Origin of Species
(1859)

- Darwin argued that certain members of a species inherit traits which over time may make them more successful in the struggle for survival.
- These traits are then passed down, while those members of the species who lack such characteristics ultimately do not reproduce.
- Darwin labeled this process "**natural selection.**"

Fallout from Darwin

The Descent of Man
(1871)

Opposition to Darwin was swift and vehement, particularly from religious groups, who saw such ideas as a direct threat to the very basis of their beliefs.

Darwin's Followers and "Survival of the Fittest"

Darwin did attract a number of followers. Although Darwin was always calculating in his own speculative thought, many of his followers pursued his ideas with wild abandon. It was Herbert Spencer (1820–1903) who first used the phrase "survival of the fittest," a phrase never in fact uttered by Darwin. For Spencer, such an idea provided justification for governments to abandon the poor; he believed that giving aid on their behalf would upset the natural order of survival. Such ideas, which received the label "Social Darwinism," were used to justify the idea that Europeans were superior to Africans and Asians and therefore should dominate them. Across Europe, ardent nationalists used the concept of survival of the fittest to explain the constant state of tensions between nations and why some states thrived while others didn't. Social Darwinism also played a role in the heightened anti-Semitism found across Europe in the last quarter of the 19th century, as some argued that Jews were a lesser race and could never be integrated within the larger fabric of society.

Social Class and the
Second Industrial Revolution 😎

Far-reaching industrial developments played a significant role in changing the social dynamic in western Europe. One group in decline was the
traditional aristocracy. The French Revolution created the concept of a
meritocracy, thereby eliminating any special privileges based on birth.
The second half of the 19th century has sometimes been called the
"Age of the Middle Class."

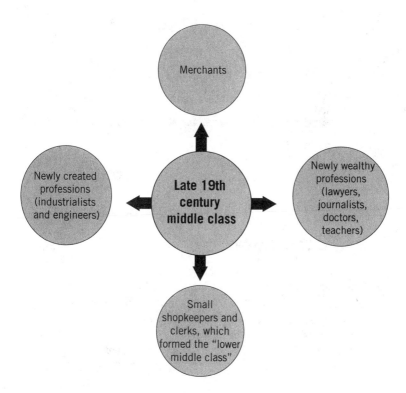

These people were "middle class" in the sense that they fell outside
the old European class system. On the whole, they were not middle-
income; they were instead quite wealthy. The late 1800s were significant not because the middle class was new, but because it was larger
than ever before.

Middle-Class Living 💬

As a group, the middle class* enjoyed new luxuries:

fresh running water
central heating
at least one servant
consumer goods
travel

Did You Know?

🔊 The Second Industrial Revolution brought about some improvements in the standard of living for the working class. One example of this is the development of popular entertainment such as dance halls and professional sports leagues, a sign that the working-class income was not entirely consumed by survival necessities, such as food and housing.

---

*Thomas Cook (1808–1892) popularized travel among the middle class when he organized day trips to the Great Exhibition in London, thus giving rise to the tourist trade. For those seeking less vigorous relaxation than seeing 10 countries in as many days, spas and resorts became common vacation destinations.

Victorian Morality 💬

Another sign that the middle class enjoyed preeminence at this time was that its standards of behavior became the societal norms.

Improvements to Life	Challenges to Life
• Certain barbaric forms of popular entertainment, such as animal fights, ceased.	• Victorian sensibilities seemed to preclude women from living fulfilled lives.
• The late Victorian period did witness the development of a women's rights movement in Great Britain and, to a lesser extent, France and Germany.	• Women were excluded from the professions and from enrollment in institutions of higher education.

The New Radicals 💬

For many in the working class across western Europe, the improved living conditions from the Second Industrial Revolution were slight at best. Many still saw socialism as the best means to change their dreary existence. However, the way that socialist goals were to be carried out had become less radical:

1. Since capitalism was such an entrenched part of life, workers found it more practical to try to attain gradual improvements in working conditions than to launch an all-out revolutionary upheaval.
2. The development of parliamentary democracy and universal male suffrage in parts of western Europe led workers to believe that socialism could be achieved through the ballot box.
3. **Eduard Bernstein** (1850–1932), a German intellectual, challenged some of Marx's basic ideas in *Evolutionary Socialism* (1899). He and his followers, who were labeled **"revisionists,"** argued that capitalism was not, as Marx claimed, about to collapse.

That said, some socialists held firm to the validity of Marx's "laws" and were harsh toward the revisionists, whom they considered heretics:

Karl Kautsky
- Czech-Austrian philosopher
- Worked closely with Engels
- Unlike Marx, he claimed that the proletarian revolution would not be a bloody affair but a civilized process.

Rosa Luxemburg
- Polish philosopher
- Critical of more moderate forms of Socialism
- Thought the era of capitalism was in its final throes and saw labor strikes and revolutionary actions as necessary to test the waters and overthrow the capitalist state

Pierre-Joseph Proudhon
- "Father of **anarchism**"
- Believed that the true laws of society had little to do with authority and came from the nature of society itself
- Wanted workers to organize small groups of independent producers that would govern themselves without interference from the state

Did You Know?

Anarchists wanted to see the state abolished. While anarchism never gained the support of as many workers as socialism, in certain regions, such as in the Spanish province of Andalusia, the movement had a significant following.

Ask Yourself...

What political consequences emerged from the Second Industrial Revolution in Europe?

Social and Cultural Developments 💬

Religion 💬

Religious beliefs and institutions made a significant recovery in the period after 1815, particularly considering the extent of the challenges posed to organized religion by the Enlightenment, the French Revolution, and the Napoleonic era. Secular rulers saw religion as an important bulwark for the existing social order, with the revolutions of 1848 further spurring this trend toward state support of religion.

Catholicism 🗨

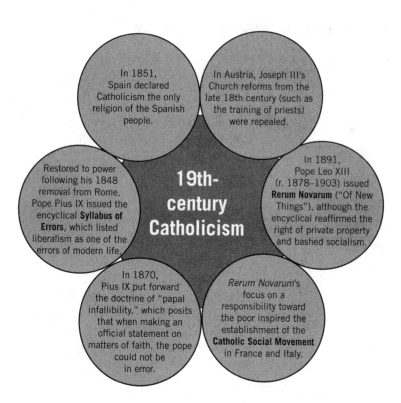

In 1851, Spain declared Catholicism the only religion of the Spanish people.

In Austria, Joseph III's Church reforms from the late 18th century (such as the training of priests) were repealed.

Restored to power following his 1848 removal from Rome, Pope Pius IX issued the encyclical **Syllabus of Errors**, which listed liberalism as one of the errors of modern life.

19th-century Catholicism

In 1891, Pope Leo XIII (r. 1878–1903) issued **Rerum Novarum** ("Of New Things"), although the encyclical reaffirmed the right of private property and bashed socialism.

In 1870, Pius IX put forward the doctrine of "papal infallibility," which posits that when making an official statement on matters of faith, the pope could not be in error.

Rerum Novarum's focus on a responsibility toward the poor inspired the establishment of the **Catholic Social Movement** in France and Italy.

The Bible as History

In the German states in the early 19th century, a group of theologians began to study the Bible as history in search of the **"historical" Jesus**. A critical step in this effort was the publication in 1835 of *The Life of Jesus, Critically Examined* by **David Friedrich Strauss** (1808–1874). For Strauss, the Bible consisted of a series of myths formulated by the early Christians, ultimately providing for a scripture that contained, in his famous phrase a "Christ of faith, rather than the Jesus of history."

Religion for the Working Class and Peasants

In Great Britain, a religious census taken in 1851 revealed that attendance at church (it assumed everyone was Christian) was much lower than expected and that the working class in particular had very little connection with organized religion.

Judaism, Anti-Semitism, and Zionism

For Jews, the 19th century presented new opportunities as well as new pressures.

Improvement in Late 19th-Century European Jewish Life

❑ In 1858, Jews were allowed to enter the House of Commons in Great Britain.
❑ Jews received full political rights in Austria-Hungary and Germany.

Challenges to Late 19th-Century European Jewish Life

❑ In many countries, Jews who wanted to rise in certain professions or in government often found the path blocked to them unless they converted to Christianity. Jews were seen as responsible for economic downturns, such as the 1873 recession.
❑ **Anti-Semitism** developed, based on Social Darwinist notions of Jews as being part of a distinct and foreign race and not just members of a religious denomination.
❑ In Russia, the monarchy used attacks on Jews, or **pogroms**, as a tool for redirecting popular anger, which might otherwise have been directed toward the throne.*
❑ France saw the rise of *Action Française*, a virulently anti-Semitic monarchist group.
❑ Politicians, such as Vienna mayor Karl Lueger (1844–1910), were elected on openly anti-Semitic platforms.
❑ Anti-Semitic political organizations, such as the far right-wing **Christian Social Party** in Germany, began to pick up steam in Europe.

---

*Several million Jews left Russia at the turn of the century to escape the persecution that grew worse after the 1905 Revolution.

A clear example of the anti-Semitism that was rampant in Europe at the turn of the century was the **Dreyfus Affair**. In 1894, a Jewish captain in the French army was accused of leaking secrets to Germany. Alfred Dreyfus was found guilty and sentenced to life in prison off French Guiana. As he was sent away, his insignia was ripped from his shirt as he was paraded before a crowd chanting "death to the Jew." When exonerating evidence was discovered, the French military tried to cover it up. French writer Émile Zola wrote a scathing letter critical of the military entitled "J'Accuse...!" for which he was convicted of libel. In 1906, Dreyfus was officially cleared of all charges; however, the Dreyfus Affair had already revealed deep divides within the French population over questions of national identity.

For many Jews, the optimism they felt at the middle of the century that the future would bring ever greater social acceptance was by the end of the 19th century being destroyed by a wave of hatred. For some, this would lead to the conclusion that the only hope to live in peace would be through the establishment of a Jewish homeland.

The leading advocate for **Zionism**, as the idea for establishing a Jewish homeland was called, was **Theodore Herzl** (1860–1904), an Austrian journalist who was horrified over the anti-Semitism that bubbled over the surface as a result of the Dreyfus Affair.

In *The Jewish State,* he argued that Jews must have a state of their own and began to form a worldwide organization to achieve this goal, with the First Zionist Congress meeting in Switzerland in 1897.

The Rights and Role of Women

The role of the family changed in the 19th century, with one of the most significant developments being that families, which at one time operated as a cohesive economic unit, no longer functioned in such a manner. Increasingly, there were now separate spheres for both male and female endeavors, with the male going off to earn the money that provided for the family's support.

Cult of Domesticity

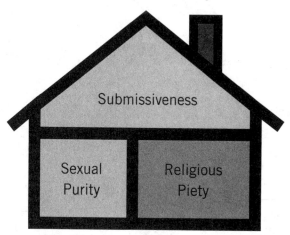

 Did You Know?

🖝 Who Is Isabella Beeton?

She wrote the most famous advice book for women during the last part of the 19th century. Her *Book of Household Management* was second in sales in Great Britain only to the Bible.

Women's Struggles for Increased Rights

As the century continued, a growing number of women began to criticize the civil disabilities under which they lived, such as the lack of right to divorce or to possess property rights. These women, who adopted the French word **"feminist"** to describe themselves, began to establish organizations to help bring about change.

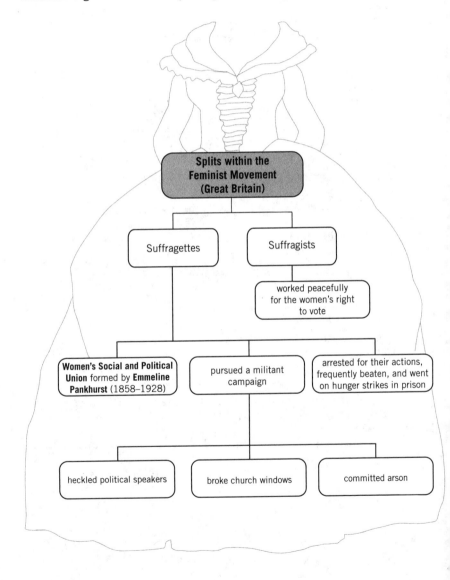

Splits within the Feminist Movement (Great Britain)

- Suffragettes
- Suffragists
  - worked peacefully for the women's right to vote

Suffragettes:
- **Women's Social and Political Union** formed by **Emmeline Pankhurst** (1858–1928)
- pursued a militant campaign
- arrested for their actions, frequently beaten, and went on hunger strikes in prison

- heckled political speakers
- broke church windows
- committed arson

Some women saw the path to equality primarily through the lens of socialism:

Clara Zetkin (1857–1933)
- Marxist
- Eschewed feminism in favor of socialism
- Saw socialism as offering women the only possibility for ending their oppression

Flora Tristan (1803–1844)
- Combined socialism and feminism
- Viewed social equality between the sexes as the path to economic equality
- Created the **Workers' Union** to achieve this goal
- Male socialists largely ignored her aims.

In 1918, women in Great Britain finally achieved the right to vote. There is ongoing historical debate regarding whether it was the suffragettes or the suffragists who ultimately deserve the credit for this momentous achievement.

Emergence of the Social Sciences 💬

In the 19th century, there was a new impetus to take the methodology established in the sciences and apply it to the workings of society.

Field	Purpose
History	The historical texts of the 19th century were seen as unreliable and instead social scientists felt that it was necessary to find trends based on primary sources.
Anthropology	European dominance over large parts of the globe as a result of the new imperialism inspired the establishment of national anthropological societies, although unfortunately, due to the "scientific" racism of the age, such societies often spent their time exploring the "inferiority" of non-Europeans.
Sociology	The study of human social behavior was in part inspired by the growing tendency of governments to keep statistics on the conditions of their citizenry.
Archaeology	Scientific principles began to be applied to the field of archaeology, which in the 19th century still remained the preserve of dedicated amateurs.

Arts ❗

Romanticism ❗

Romanticism began in the second half of the 18th century as a rejection of what was viewed as the cold rationalism of 18th-century Neoclassicism and instead placed a much higher value on the primacy of emotions and feeling.

Examples of Romanticism in Music

Ludwig von Beethoven

Franz Schubert

Hector Berlioz

Frederic Chopin

Igor Stravinsky

Franz Liszt

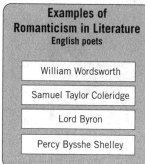

Examples of Romanticism in Literature
English poets

William Wordsworth

Samuel Taylor Coleridge

Lord Byron

Percy Bysshe Shelley

Examples of Romanticism in Literature
Novelists

Sir Walter Scott

Johann Wolfgang von Goethe

Victor Hugo

Did You Know?

Some composers made use of traditional oral tales or folk songs: **Frederic Chopin** (1810–1849) was influenced by the music of the peasants of his native Poland, and **Franz Liszt** (1811–1886) composed pieces based on traditional gypsy music.

Romanticism vs. Realism ❗

In the visual arts, Romantic artists often attempted to capture the feeling and power of nationalism. A key example of this is **Eugène Delacroix's** (1798–1863) *Liberty Leading the People*, which was painted one year after the overthrow of Charles X and captures the stirring events of the revolution in the streets of Paris.

Some artists began to look to new subjects, such as those we refer to as the **realists**, who sought to paint the world around them without any illusions. In part inspired by the revolutionary upheavals of 1848, **Gustave Courbet** (1819–1877) began to paint works like *The Stone Breakers* that rejected the romantic traditions of the day and instead focused on showing the world of the peasants in all its grim reality.

Jean-François Millet (1814–1875) is most famous for *The Sower*, which shows hardscrabble peasants who seem, like the wheat, to be growing out of the earth. Millet was himself from the peasant class and refused to paint them in an idealistic manner, nor did he seek to show that hard labor brought happiness.

Realism in Literature 🔔

Realism was also an important movement in literature. Just as realist painters wanted to show the world the actual conditions of those on the bottom of the social order, so too did novelists.

Examples of Realist Authors in Literature

Honoré de Balzac
Charles Dickens
George Eliot
Gustave Flaubert
Leo Tolstoy
Fyodor Dostoyevsky
Émile Zola

 The Genius of Picasso

The most revolutionary artist of the 20th century was Pablo Picasso, who, with his nearly abstract *Les Demoiselles d'Avignon* (1907), made an irreparable break with the single-point perspective that had been central to Western art since the time of the Italian Renaissance. Later on, Picasso became famous as the cofounder (with Georges Braque) of Cubism.

 Ask Yourself...

- How did the role of religion in European society change during the 19th century?
- What specific events in history can you tie to a movement in art or literature that emerged during the 19th century?

The New Imperialism ❗

In the 1880s, the nations of Europe began an expansion into Africa and Asia that was unprecedented both for its speed and its scale. This period of conquest, along with the establishment of colonies, is referred to as the **"new imperialism."** The term is used not only to separate this period from earlier periods of overseas conquest, such as the Spanish conquest of Central and South America, but also to denote the fundamental ways in which life was transformed in those regions that were now under the sway of Europeans.

The Technology that Made It Possible ❗

The new imperialism was built on a foundation of **technological advances:**

- Breech-loading rifles, which allowed the user to fire from a prone position, offered a significant advantage over the muzzle loaders still in use by those Africans who had guns. Even greater firepower was provided by the introduction of rapid-fire weapons such as the Gatling gun.
- Steamships allowed for rapid transport across oceans without having to deal with the vagaries of wind power, and smaller steam-driven river boats allowed Europeans to penetrate into the heart of Africa. The construction of the Suez Canal, which was finished in 1869, significantly reduced the time it took to go from Europe to Asia.
- One of the most important technological developments for imperialism was the telegraph, which allowed for the exchange of messages between India and London over the course of a day—a dramatic decrease over the two years it took at the start of the century.
- The discovery in 1820 of quinine, a drug made from the bark of the cinchona tree, was an effective treatment for the great scourge of the tropics—malaria.

Social Imperialists ❗

Although technology was vital for the new imperialism, it would have made little difference without the various motivating factors that stirred Europeans to conquer foreign lands. One important factor was the search for profits that were assumed to be had from imperialism. Yet those imperialists who saw colonies as a source of unimaginable wealth were going to be disappointed, because many colonies lacked any economic value*. Other motivating factors came from **social imperialists**, who viewed imperialism as a means of relieving certain domestic social problems.

Nationalism	• Nationalism played a major role in empire building. • European states believed that the only way they could matter on a global scale would be through the establishment of colonies.
Religion	• Christian missionaries were actually the first Europeans to penetrate central Africa.
Balance of Power	• Balance of power was the most significant reason for the acquisition of even unprofitable pieces of land. • Nations wanted colonies so that the other nations would not get them. • **Cecil Rhodes** (Great Britain) attempted to gain colonial advantage from the Cape of Good Hope to Cairo.

---

*The exception to this was India, where the British were able to extract enough wealth for it to be justifiably referred to as the "jewel in the crown."

Mad Scramble ❗

In what has become known as the **"mad scramble"** for colonies, Europeans drew new borders that demonstrated their lack of concern for tribal and cultural differences with imperial territories.

Africa ❗

The 1884 **Berlin Conference** ultimately set up rules for the establishment of colonies in Africa. The outcome of that conference is shown on the map below:

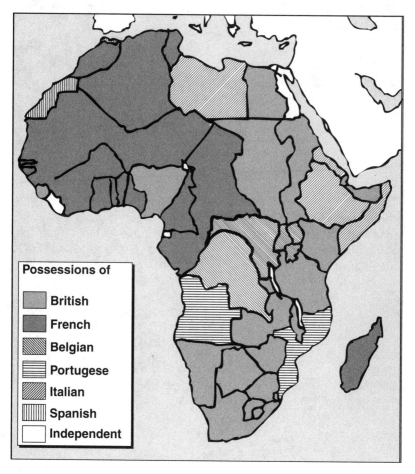

Possessions of

- British
- French
- Belgian
- Portugese
- Italian
- Spanish
- Independent

Did You Know?

🗨 There were two exceptions in Africa to the mad scramble: **Ethiopia**, which repelled an Italian invasion in 1896, and the small state of **Liberia** on the west coast of Africa, which remained independent as a result of its unique historical link to the United States.

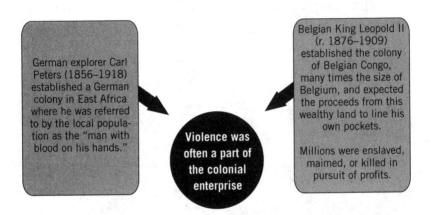

German explorer Carl Peters (1856–1918) established a German colony in East Africa where he was referred to by the local population as the "man with blood on his hands."

Violence was often a part of the colonial enterprise

Belgian King Leopold II (r. 1876–1909) established the colony of Belgian Congo, many times the size of Belgium, and expected the proceeds from this wealthy land to line his own pockets.

Millions were enslaved, maimed, or killed in pursuit of profits.

King Leopold II was the "Butcher of the Congo," leaving a body count equal to that of the Nazis. He depopulated villages, devastated wildlife, ransacked the land for gold, chopped off hands and feet, and murdered millions. The country—the size of 76 Belgiums—"belonged" to Leopold and Leopold alone. After the district governors took their commission, he kept 100% of the profits.

India ❗

British dominance over **India** began to take shape following the withdrawal of the French from the Indian subcontinent as a result of the Seven Years' War (1756-1763). As the 19th century continued, additional, formerly independent Indian territories fell under British control.

> 1877: Prime Minister Disraeli made Queen Victoria the Empress of India, which issued a warning to the other European powers concerning the significance of India for Great Britain.

Punjab region fell under British control in 1849.

The **Sepoy Rebellion** of 1857 (or **"Indian Mutiny"** as the British called it) occurred when Indians fought to remove the British colonial presence.

After the rebellion was put down, colonial control became more centralized with the establishment of an administrative structure to replace the British East India Company.

China ❗

In **China,** Great Britain was the first European state to practice what is referred to as **"informal empire,"** in which a state has significant influence over another nation's economy without actual territorial or political control.

China loses a series of wars with Great Britain in the second half of the 19th century (the Opium Wars).

China grants European states soverign control over a series of "treaty ports" along the coast.

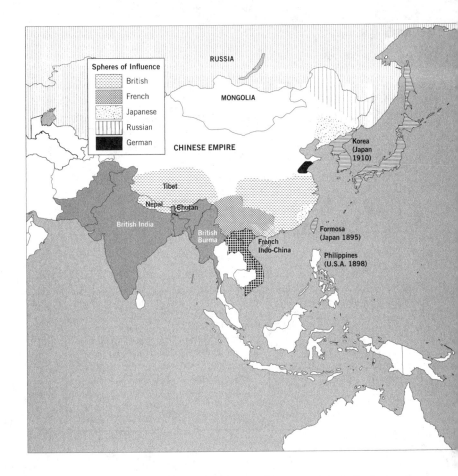

Spheres of Influence
- British
- French
- Japanese
- Russian
- German

RUSSIA

MONGOLIA

CHINESE EMPIRE

Korea (Japan 1910)

Tibet

Nepal Bhutan

British India

British Burma

French Indo-China

Formosa (Japan 1895)

Philippines (U.S.A. 1898)

In Southeast Asia, although Thailand was able to maintain its independence, the French seized control of **Indochina** (which you may know by its current name, Vietnam) and its vital rubber plantations.

 Did You Know?

🌀 **Japan**, which had imitated Britain and Germany in its economic transformation into an industrial power, would also mimic their taste for colonial expansion by seizing control of **Korea** in 1910, five years after the end of the **Russo-Japanese War.**

What Did Colonized Nations Get Out of the Deal?

Colonialism could also provide certain benefits for the colonized nation.

- **Infrastructure** The British invested in irrigation systems, railways, and cities in India.
- **Nationalism** The concepts of nationalism and political liberty (both European exports) were later used by colonial peoples as a tool for their own liberation.*

Views and Consequences of the New Imperialism

While much support in Europe for imperialism rested with the *mission civilisatrice* (civilizing mission), international conflicts stemming from imperial pursuits did not always go over well back on the home front. In recent years, historians have asked whether imperialism was ever actually popular among the mass of population, and the question has not been fully answered.

 Did You Know?

Elements of imperialism can be found in Rudyard Kipling's "The White Man's Burden" (1899), in which he writes that Europeans have a moral obligation to "bind your sons to exile/To serve your captives' need."

---

*Africans and Asians who had the most contact with the West, often through study abroad in Europe, were the most committed nationalists.

Enthusiasm for imperialism

Newspapers filled their pages with colonial exploits

In Germany, the **Pan-German League,** a far right-wing group, called for imperialsm as a way to unify Germans under a common national goal

In Britain, the pro-imperial Primrose League had more than a million members

Weariness of imperialism

The **Boer War** (1899–1902) between the British Empire and Dutch descendants in South Africa

Heightened tensions among the European powers following British establishment of a de facto protectorate over Egypt and the Suez Canal in 1882

A British and Russian struggle over the generally worthless territory of Afghanistan in what was referred to as the **"great game"**

Near war between Great Britain and France over **Fashoda** in the Sudan in 1898

Did You Know?

Otto von Bismarck showed little interest in colonies. He once famously displayed this lack of interest by pointing to a map of Europe and stating, "This is my Africa" to show his true object of fascination.

Resistance to Imperialism

While many of Europe's leaders pursued colonies in Africa and Asia, their efforts were met with considerable resistance from a number of different directions, from European dissidents to African and Asian nationalists:

From Socialists
- British economist **J.A. Hobson** and Russian political theorist Vladimir Lenin, both Marxists, opposed imperialism as an outgrowth of capitalism.

From Colonized Peoples
- The **Indian Congress Party** was created in 1885 to resist Great Britain's colonial presence on the Indian subcontinent.
- The **Zulu Resistance** saw native people from South Africa use military tactics to oppose European colonizers.
- The 1899 **Boxer Rebellion** in China aimed to remove Christian missionaries and Western businesses.

Opposition to Imperialism

In Literature
- French author **Jules Verne**'s works *Twenty Thousand Leagues Under the Sea* (1870) and *The Mysterious Island* (1874) feature an ardently anti-imperialist character named Captain Nemo.
- British author **Joseph Conrad**'s novella *Heart of Darkness* (1899) slowly uncovers the evils inherent in the colonial settlements of the Congo.

From Reformers
- British journalist E.D. Morel, horrified by the conditions set up by King Leopold in the Congo, created the **Congo Reform Association** to bring worldwide attention to the inhumanity present in the Belgian colony.

Ask Yourself...

In what ways did the motivations and outcomes of the New Imperialism differ from that of the conquests of the 15th and 16th centuries?

Year(s)	Event
1717	Abraham Darby smelts iron using partially burnt coal
1733	John Kay's flying shuttle
1764	James Hargreaves's spinning jenny
1769	Richard Arkwright patents the water frame
1774	James Watt patents the first steam engine
1776	Adam Smith's *An Inquiry into the Nature and Causes of the Wealth of Nations*
1779	First iron bridge completed in Shropshire, England
1785	Power loom invented by Edmund Cartwright
1789	Jeremy Bentham's *Introduction to the Principles of Morals and Legislation*
1790	Burke's *Reflections on the Revolution in France*
1793	Eli Whitney's cotton gin
1798	Thomas Malthus's *Essay on Population*
1807	British Parliament votes for the end of the slave trade
1807	First passenger train line
1815	Napoleon escapes from Elba (March 15)
1815	Battle of Waterloo marks end of the Hundred Days' War (May 15)
1815	Napoleon sent into exile on St. Helena
1817	David Ricardo's *Principles of Political Economy*

Year(s)	Event
1819	Peterloo Massacre in Great Britain
1819	Combination Acts ban union activity
1820	Troppau Protocol (agreement among Eastern Great Powers to oppose revolutionary states)
1820	Rebellion in Spain put down with French support in 1824
1821	Beginning of Greek revolt
1821	Death of Napoleon
1823	Revolt in Naples
1824	Charles X becomes King of France
1825	Decembrist revolt in Russia
1829	George Stephenson invents the early locomotive, the Rocket
1830	Charles X issues July Ordinances
1830	July Revolution topples the last French Bourbon monarch
1830s	Cholera outbreak in Europe
1831	Charles Darwin leaves on five-year voyage that will take him to the Galapagos Islands
1832	Sadler Committee looks into child labor in Great Britain
1832	Great Reform Bill
1833	Slavery banned within the British empire
1833	Factory Act

Year(s)	Event
1833	English Poor Law
1834	Robert Owen establishes the Grand National Consolidated Union
1835	David Friedrich Strauss's *The Life of Jesus Critically Examined*
1835	Daguerreotype (early form of photograph) invented
1837	Beginning of the reign of Queen Victoria
1838	Beginning of the Chartist movement
1839	First in a series of Opium Wars between Great Britain and China
1840	Napoleon's body brought back to France for reburial
1840	Joseph Proudhon writes the anarchist tract "What Is Property?"
1842	British gain control over Hong Kong
1846	Repeal of the Corn Laws
1846	Irish potato famine
1847	Liberia established as independent African republic
1848	*The Communist Manifesto* by Karl Marx and Friedrich Engels (February)
1848	Overthrow of Louis Philippe (February)
1848	Unrest in various German states (March)

Year(s)	Event
1848	Nationalist revolts break out throughout Austrian Empire (beginning in March)
1848	Charles Albert of Savoy goes to war against Austria (March)
1848	Meeting of the Frankfurt Parliament (May)
1848	"June Days" uprising in Paris
1848	Louis Napoleon elected president of the Second Republic (December)
1851	Louis Napoleon stages coup against the Second Republic Crystal Palace exhibition
1852	Development of the safety elevator
1852	David Livingstone begins exploring the African interior
1852	Commodore Perry arrives in Japan
1852	Establishment of the Second Empire by Napoleon III
1854	Charles Dickens publishes *Hard Times*
1854	Start of the Crimean War
1856	Development of Bessemer process for manufacturing steel
1856	Synthetic dyes developed
1857	Flaubert publishes his masterpiece, *Madame Bovary*
1857	Indian Rebellion

Year(s)	Event
1858	Jews allowed to enter the British Parliament
1859	Darwin's *On the Origin of Species*
1859	France and Piedmont-Sardinia go to war against Austria
1859	Garibaldi invades the Kingdom of Two Sicilies
1861	Victor Emmanuel II becomes the first King of Italy
1861	Alexander II emancipates the serfs
1863	Opening of the Salon des Refusés (art rejected by the jury of the Official Paris Salon)
1864	Establishment of the First International in London
1864	Prussia and Austria go to war against Denmark
1866	Italians seize Venetia from Austria
1866	Austro-Prussian War
1867	Establishment of the Austro-Hungarian Empire
1867	Alfred Nobel patents dynamite
1869	Suez Canal completed
1869	John Stuart Mill's *On Liberty*
1870	Doctrine of Papal Infallibility
1870	Rome becomes capital of Italy
1870	Franco-Prussian War

Year(s)	Event
1870	French Third Republic created
1871	Establishment of the German Empire
1871	End of the French Second Empire
1871	Paris Commune
1871	Darwin's *The Descent of Man*
1874	Typewriters invented
1874	Claude Monet paints *Impression: Sunrise*
1875	Constitution establishes the French Third Republic
1876	Serbia becomes independent
1876	Alexander Graham Bell's telephone
1877	Thomas Edison's phonograph
1877	Queen Victoria becomes empress of India
1877	Russo-Turkish War
1878	Congress of Berlin
1879	Dual Alliance between Germany and Austria-Hungary
1879	Thomas Edison invents the incandescent lamp
1881	Assassination of Alexander II
1882	Great Britain seizes control over the Egyptian government

Year(s)	Event
1884	Berlin Conference
1885	Introduction of the internal combustion engine
1885	First meeting of the Indian National Congress
1885	Friedrich Nietzsche's *Thus Spake Zarathustra*
1887	Reinsurance Treaty between Germany and Russia
1890	Kaiser Wilhelm II forces Bismarck to retire as Chancellor
1890	Germany fails to renew Reinsurance Treaty
1891	Pope Leo XIII issues Rerum Novarum
1894	Beginning of the Dreyfus Affair
1894	Russo-Japanese War
1894	Russian-French alliance
1896	Italians defeated by the Ethiopians at the Battle of Adwa
1897	First Zionist Congress meets in Switzerland
1898	Eduard Bernstein publishes *Evolutionary Socialism*
1898	Spanish-American War
1898	France and Britain almost go to war over incident at Fashoda
1899	Start of the Boer War
1900	Sigmund Freud's *The Interpretation of Dreams*

Year(s)	Event
1901	Max Planck introduces quantum physics
1902	J. A. Hobson's *Imperialism: A Study*
1903	Emmeline Pankhurst forms the Women's Social and Political Union
1903	First successful airplane flight by the Wright brothers
1904	Herero War
1904	British-French entente (Entente Cordiale)
1905	Revolution in Russia leads to granting of a Duma
1905	First Moroccan Crisis
1905	Separation of church and state in France
1906	*HMS Dreadnought* launched
1907	British-Russian entente
1908	Henry Ford's Model T
1908	Austria-Hungary annexes Bosnia
1910	Madame Curie isolates radium
1911	Agadir Crisis in Morocco (aka Second Moroccan Crisis)
1913	Sergei Diaghilev revolutionizes ballet with *The Rite of Spring*
1913	Socialists become largest political party in Germany

CHAPTER 4

Global Wars to Globalization: c. 1914–Present

Laying the Tracks !

How do you go about kicking off a global war? Well, first you need a bunch of people who can fight the war, and in Europe those were the five great powers, the **Pentarchy**.

The next thing you need is some agitation, and all of the great powers were in a situation of internal discontent to some degree. There were some Europe-wide trends that also contributed. One was increasing **militarization**; European states were building more and better weapons, spending more money on their militaries, and becoming increasingly willing to resort to military solutions to complex problems. Moreover, war was valorized as a testing ground for honor and manliness, a sort of chivalrous exercise that resembled a football game rather than an actual war. People thought that everyone would come together in a quick heroic skirmish, their side would win, and all the problems and arguments stressing everyone out would be solved. If that was how people thought about war, it's no wonder that avoiding one wasn't a super high priority.

Mo' Colonies, Mo' Problems 💀

The sun never set on the British Empire, the greatest colonial power of the era. As it turns out, though, empires are expensive—especially if Imperial Germany wanted to spend an enormous amount of money on building a fleet that could sink your fleet and take all your colonies in case of war. To respond to the German naval challenge, the British government accelerated their own shipbuilding, but capital ships were very expensive (especially after the launch of **HMS Dreadnought** in 1906).

HMS Dreadnought was the first battleship to be powered by steam turbines and to mount an all-big-gun armament of ten 12-inch guns, and was thus both the fastest and the best-armed battleship in the world when it was launched. It made all other battleships, which would soon be called "pre-dreadnoughts" obsolete. Dreadnoughts (ships like *HMS Dreadnought*) were very powerful, but also incredibly expensive. By 1914, Britain had built over 20 Dreadnoughts and Super-Dreadnoughts.

All the money to build these battleships had to come from somewhere, and it came from increasing taxes on wealthy Britons and decreasing social services provided to poor Britons, increasing poverty and leading to substantial growth in labor unrest in Britain.

Britain was also facing substantial problems in its oldest and closest colony, Ireland. Irish **Nationalists** (overwhelmingly Catholic) increasingly agitated for independence from Great Britain, while smaller numbers of Irish **Unionists** (overwhelmingly Protestant) wished to remain part of Great Britain. Nationalists fought British police and Unionists in a low-grade civil conflict not finally resolved until the late 20th century.

The French National Sport

Alfred Dreyfus (1859–1935)

France was, as usual, internally divided. Secularists, Catholics, Republicans, Monarchists, Socialists, and others engaged in bitter disputes in parliament and coffeehouses and fields across France. The **Third Republic** had only come into existence in 1870 following Napoleon III's defeat in the Franco-Prussian War, and its divisions were substantially worsened by the scandal that came to be known as the Dreyfus Affair, which we talked about way back on page 158.

The Giant with Clay Feet

While Russia remained very big, it faced some equally big problems. Its brutal, inefficient government was led by the not-very-bright **Nicholas II**, and the vast majority of Russians lived as illiterate peasants, just as they had in the 17th century. Urban centers in European Russia produced much of Russia's industrial output, but were also full of poverty-stricken workers. Much of the Russian intellectual class opposed the government, with anarchism and socialism as the most popular alternatives. Secret societies and anarchist groups bombed government buildings and assassinated officials, while the Romanov secret police arrested, imprisoned, and executed people regularly.

Pyotr Stolypin, appointed Interior Minister in 1906, was so infamously repressive that the hangman's noose became known as a Stolypin Necktie. He survived 10 assassination attempts before being fatally wounded in an 11th in September 1911.

❗ The **Russo-Japanese War** of 1904–1905 most clearly exposed Russian weakness. The two empires were both expanding into East Asia and clashed over who would dominate Korea and eastern China. Japan started the war with a sneak attack on the Russian Far East fleet, at anchor in the fortified naval base of Port Arthur, and followed up with a land invasion. Though the fighting was heavy and losses were high on both sides, the Japanese won every major battle both at land and at sea, and the peace treaty recognized Japanese control over Korea and Manchuria.

The impact of the Russian defeat was made substantially worse by widespread European racism. European powers had become so used to having an insurmountable technological edge over their non-European opponents that the very idea that Japan could win was inconceivable in Europe before it happened.

❗ Russian defeat led to internal unrest, culminating in the **Russian Revolution of 1905**. This was a wave of demonstrations, strikes, peasant uprisings, and military mutinies involving clashes with police and loyal military units that left over 10,000 people dead. To stem the tide, Nicholas II felt forced to yield to many of the revolutionary demands. He signed the **October Manifesto** in October 1905, creating a Russian Parliament (the **Duma**), granting some civil rights, legalizing political parties, and expanding Russian voting rights.

Ask Yourself...

Did military defeat and internal unrest force the Tsar to set up some form of democracy and civil rights?

The Homeland of European Socialism?

The German Empire had very rapidly become the continent's leading industrial power, with a rapidly growing and highly educated population. The Reichstag, the German federal parliament, was quite democratic and wielded important powers, but the Emperor controlled the army and foreign policy. After 1888, the German Emperor was **Wilhelm II Hohenzollern**, who, like his Russian cousin, was quite conservative and not very competent. He drew much of his support from rich industrialists, the traditional aristocratic caste (**Junkers**), and the army. However, Germany's industrial and scientific strength also supercharged the population's demands for better treatment, better living conditions, and more say over their government, and Germany was also home to the largest and most powerful socialist movement in the world. In the 1912 elections, the **Social Democratic Party** (SPD) won a third of the seats in the Reichstag and became the largest political party in Germany, and it was constantly fighting with the Emperor.

However, most people in Imperial Germany wanted their country to have a place in the sun. Germany didn't even exist until 1871, but now it was the leading industrial power in Europe, full of inventions and art and progress and people! Yet with all that, they didn't have any colonies, or much of a navy, or the kind of respect and power on the world stage that Germans thought they deserved. Much of Wilhelmine policy was, on some level, an attempt to solve this problem.

 Ask Yourself...

Did the conflict between social democracy and authoritarian militarism define Germany's internal politics?

How Many Nations Is Too Many Nations?

Austria-Hungary had never been the most stable place in Europe, but the biggest problem facing the Habsburgs in the late 19th century was the growth of various nationalist movements. When the **Compromise of 1867** turned the Habsburg Empire into Austria-Hungary, the idea was more or less that Germans would govern the Austrian half and Hungarians would rule the Hungarian half. The problem was that Germans and Hungarians together were only about a third of the population, and the rest were Czechs, Slovaks, Romanians, Italians, Serbs, Bosnians, Bulgarians, Roma, Croats, and others.* This worked fine when nobody considered nationalism to be super important, but once it did become important, it caused all sorts of problems. For instance, Serb nationalists wanted the areas in which they lived to become part of Serbia, while Italian nationalists wanted Austria-Hungary's Italian-speaking areas to become part of Italy. Even many Austrians, especially in the border regions, wanted to become part of Imperial Germany. Nationalities without foreign homelands wanted independence, and some people in those movements were happy to work with foreign powers to bring that about. Some even resorted to terrorism. For more on that, keep reading!

Imagine how difficult it was to organize a society in which everything had to be communicated in 13 different languages! This was one cause of the inefficiency that Austria-Hungary was famous for.

Building the War Train ⚠️

Problems in domestic affairs contributed to the outbreak of the First World War, but foreign affairs also played an important role. One problem was the growth of **entangling alliances**. Treaties were hardly new, but after the Franco-Prussian War of 1870–1871, Otto von Bismarck set about establishing a set of permanent peacetime alliances that would prevent France from being able to defeat Germany in the next war.

The first piece was the **Dual Alliance** with Austria-Hungary, signed in 1879, which committed both powers to going to war if either were attacked. The Kingdom of Italy became part of this alliance in 1882, creating the **Triple Alliance**. In 1887, Bismarck also negotiated the secret **Reinsurance Treaty** with Russia, which said that neither of the two

---

 *Most of the inhabitants of Austria-Hungary wanted to be part of a different country, which caused lots of problems!

would fight each other, since Russia was getting worried about the Triple Alliance. However, Bismarck was tossed overboard when Wilhelm II came to power and the Reinsurance Treaty ended in 1890.

France and Russia were alone in this new world, and it was tough not having any friends. So they decided to be friends with each other.* The **Franco-Russian Alliance** was signed in 1894, committing both powers to fight in defense of the other. The last great power, Great Britain, had spent a century refusing to sign alliances with anybody, a policy they called **Splendid Isolation**. However, once Germany started building tons of dreadnoughts, isolation started to seem like maybe a bad idea. As a result, Britain signed a series of agreements with France resolving many of their colonial disputes in 1904, which generally marks the beginning of the **Entente Cordiale**. This wasn't a military alliance or anything, but it did bring the two countries together and set the stage for informal military discussions and cooperation. Britain signed a similar agreement with Russia in 1907, the **Anglo-Russian Convention**, thus creating the **Triple Entente**.

The main problem the Triple Entente caused was that any argument between two powers suddenly became an argument between all of the great powers! You couldn't just ignore the issue like you could before. A little argument in a European backwater could blow everything up.

One such backwater was the Balkans. The Ottoman retreat over the 19th century ceded independence to Serbia, Montenegro, Bulgaria, Greece, and Romania, and had granted Austria-Hungary the right to occupy and administer Bosnia-Herzegovina. In 1908, Austria-Hungary finally decided to annex the area, in a move that caused a minor diplomatic scandal and really annoyed the Serbians, who wanted it for themselves. Everybody wanted more territory. In 1912, Serbia, Montenegro, Bulgaria, and Greece formed an alliance to attack the Ottomans and conquer the rest of Turkey's Balkan territory in the **First Balkan War**. They were successful, ending the war in victory in early 1913. However, arguments over who got what started the **Second Balkan War** of 1913. The Bulgarians wanted more and ended up with less after losing the war, while Serbia nearly doubled in size.

---

* This relationship was actually super weird! France was a revolutionary republic, while Russia was a despotic empire—hardly natural allies. When the Franco-Russian Alliance was signed, the French national anthem was actually illegal in Russia, so they had to change the law so they could play it for the ceremony.

Fresh off this great success, Serbia's government started scheming about how to seize Bosnia-Herzegovina as well, leading us to...

The Little Assassin Who Could

The specific incident that kicked off the war was the assassination of **Archduke Franz Ferdinand,** who was next in line for the throne of Austria-Hungary. A series of army maneuvers were scheduled to take place in Bosnia in June 1914, and Franz Ferdinand took the opportunity to visit Sarajevo (Bosnia's capital) to shake hands, kiss babies, and throw a parade.

Serbian military intelligence thought this was a great opportunity to kill the heir to the throne, and so they put their best man on it.

Colonel Dragutin Dimitrijević was the leader of a secret terrorist organization called the **Black Hand,** operating under his code name, Apis. Sounds scary! But as it happened the team of crack Black Hand assassins Apis sent to kill the Archduke were dimwitted high-school students with no training or experience and low-quality weapons. Their main virtues for Serbia were that they were easily manipulated and could easily be disavowed.

The Start of World War I 🛑

The Domino Effect 🛑

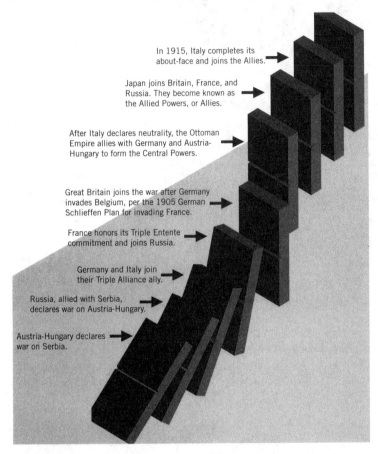

In 1915, Italy completes its about-face and joins the Allies.

Japan joins Britain, France, and Russia. They become known as the Allied Powers, or Allies.

After Italy declares neutrality, the Ottoman Empire allies with Germany and Austria-Hungary to form the Central Powers.

Great Britain joins the war after Germany invades Belgium, per the 1905 German Schlieffen Plan for invading France.

France honors its Triple Entente commitment and joins Russia.

Germany and Italy join their Triple Alliance ally.

Russia, allied with Serbia, declares war on Austria-Hungary.

Austria-Hungary declares war on Serbia.

On June 28, 1914, the day of the parade in Sarajevo, the team tried and failed to kill the Archduke several times that day. **Gavrilo Princip**, one of the assassins, had given up on trying to kill the apparently invincible Archduke and went into a shop to get a sandwich. He came out eating it, only to see the Archduke's car stalled in the street right in front of him. Astounded by his luck, he pulled out his pistol and fatally wounded both the Archduke and his wife.

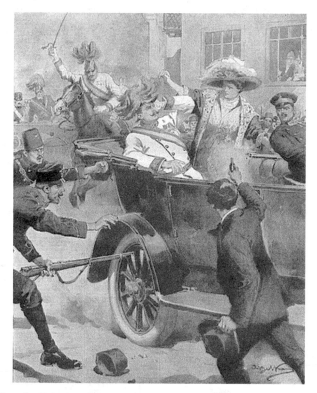

Gavrilo Princip killing Archduke Francis Ferdinand of Austria in Sarajevo by Achille Beltrame

Ask Yourself...

If you were to be asked why the First World War happened, what would be your response?

So why did Germany declare war so quickly? Well, Germany's war plan, called the **Schlieffen Plan** after its author, Alfred von Schlieffen, involved beating France quickly by circling around the forts on the border and invading through Belgium. The idea was that Russia was so big and slow that France could be beaten before Russia managed to get all of its conscripts from their villages to the border; then all the German soldiers who had just beaten France could pivot to Russia. Unfortunately for Germany, Britain had signed a treaty guaranteeing Belgium's independence in 1839, so when Germany invaded Belgium, Britain declared war on Germany. All of this took place between July 28, 1914, and August 4, 1914.

 ## *Did You Know?*

The international socialist movement had previously agreed to start general strikes across Europe in opposition to a general European war, reasoning that if all the workers stopped working, then the war couldn't happen. However, once the war actually started to happen, most of them changed their minds. The one who didn't, the Frenchman Jean Jaurès, was assassinated by a French nationalist on July 31, 1914.

Britain's entry into the war might have been worth it if France had indeed fallen, but the German effort fell just short. The French Army, with help from the British Expeditionary Force, managed to stop the Germans near Paris at the **First Battle of the Marne.***

With the lines stabilized, the various armies started digging in and the war became all about trench warfare. The technological improvements in firepower had not been matched by improvements in communications or armor, so while artillery, machine guns, and accurate long-range rifles all made it very easy to kill tons of soldiers very quickly, there really wasn't any good way to advance under fire—a situation of **superiority of the defense**. As a consequence, tens of millions of men lived in squalid conditions in muddy trenches under near-constant artillery fire, waiting for the officers to order an offensive. Attacks involved a lot of soldiers running out of their trenches and toward the opposing trenches, and all the machine guns and rifles and artillery tried to stop them. It generally went about as well as you'd expect, and was a brutal miserable life the rest of the time. The combatants tried a bunch of things to change this basic dynamic, but without much success.

---

 *French Field Marshal **Philippe Pétain** made his reputation during this battle, refusing to panic even in the face of utter defeat. He mobilized local reinforcements and brought them to the fighting front by hiring every taxi in Paris, bringing enough men to prevent further German advances. The taxi drivers later sent a bill for their services.

Some of the things tried during World War I were absolutely ridiculous, such as this suit of French body armor.

Britain, for example, tried to leverage its naval superiority to go around the Western Front and knock Turkey out of the war. This was the brainchild of then-First Lord of the Admiralty Winston Churchill, and the amphibious assault at **Gallipoli** in 1915 went so poorly it nearly ended his career. The Germans tried using artillery shells full of poison gas to get through trench lines (first against the Russians in January 1915 and then on the Western Front in April 1915) but rapid deployment of gas masks and Allied use of poison gas of their own returned the Western Front to stalemate. Eventually both sides decided that the only way to win was through attrition. Germany tried this first, in early 1916, at the siege of **Verdun**, a French military fortress of no real strategic value which they thought the French could be drawn into defending under unfavorable conditions. A lot of people died, but it turned out to be about even, so the attack failed even on its own terms. The British and French had a similar idea, and the **Battle of the Somme**, which began in July 1916, caused a million casualties on both sides—one of the bloodiest battles in human history. This battle also saw Britain deploying a new weapon, the **tank**, although the early versions were incredibly unreliable and slow.

1917 was the year that broke armies. The most important collapse was Russian, prompted not by defeat particularly (the **Brusilov Offensive** of late 1916 against Austria-Hungary was actually quite successful), but by the economic strain of supporting the war leading to internal revolution. More on that in a minute! However, the French Army also underwent a kind of mutiny. After the failure of the **Nivelle Offensive**, in spring 1917, large numbers of French troops refused to engage in offensive action. The incredible losses sustained over the war had become unsustainable. Though eventually some limited operations were undertaken in 1918, the French Army was at least temporarily broken. Last and least important, the Italian Army suffered a catastrophic defeat at the **Battle of Caporetto** in 1917 attempting to invade Austria and broke completely—no more significant Italian actions took place until the end of the war.

Since the war became such an endurance trial, the so-called **Home Front** became incredibly important. What this meant was that the ability of the national economy and population to produce men and weapons, and the willingness of the civilian population to continue to do so, became just as or even more important than whether the military won or lost any particular battle. Thus, in each of the major combatants, censorship offices and propaganda ministries demonized the enemy and encouraged ever greater efforts in the factory, field, and home to support the soldiers in the field.* Governments took over for heavily regulated economies, rationing goods from cotton to leather to dyes to horses to coal to make sure that the military could get what it needed.

Different countries faced different problems. France lost much of its industrial heartland to German conquest in the initial months of the war and spent the equivalent of over four hundred billion dollars in today's dollars on the war effort, bankrupting the country and taking out huge sums in loans primarily from the United States. Great Britain was similarly forced to liquidate enormous sums to pay for its war effort and support its allies, eventually running out of money. Most estimates of the cost of the war to Great Britain are somewhere around what would be eight hundred billion dollars today.

---

 *A theme for every single combatant's propaganda was how they were fighting a purely defensive war forced on them by enemy aggression. A strange phenomenon!

Germany and Austria-Hungary faced limitations in materials, not just money. The most important problem was food. Obviously they couldn't buy food from Russia after the war started, and the British Navy almost immediately established a very effective and quite illegal **Hunger Blockade**, preventing the Central Powers from buying anything from foreign markets. Shortages quickly appeared, and starvation was a serious risk, especially for the urban poor. By the end of the war, domestic conditions were dreadful, with millions of people barely getting enough food to survive. In 1918 Vienna, for example, the food ration for a civilian worker provided only about 700 calories per day.

The War Outside of Europe 😛

This was indeed a World War, and its impact stretched far beyond Europe's borders. Much of the world was ruled from a European capital, and both France and Britain drew heavily on their colonies for men and supplies. Japan joined the war mostly as a pretext to seize German colonies, but the Ottoman Empire sought to use the war as a tool of internal regeneration. It did not, however, turn out that way. Despite some local victories, such as the defense of Gallipoli, the Arab populations under Ottoman rule rose up in revolt, spurred on by British financial and intelligence support. Ottoman forces also perpetrated the largest atrocity of the war in the **Armenian Genocide**. Over a million Armenians were systematically deported from the Ottoman heartland in Anatolia and then systematically massacred in 1915.

Better Red Than Dead 😛

Imperial Russia was the first country to crack under the strain. It was the most underdeveloped economically and socially, with the lowest level of bureaucratic efficiency, and the hardships of the war effort—most importantly the difficulties in providing food to the cities—caused massive unrest. Fifteen million farmers had become soldiers, supply shipments to the army overstressed and eventually crippled the Russian transportation network, and supplying the cities became nearly impossible by the end of 1916.

Grigori Rasputin
(1869–1916)

Tsar Nicholas II was already a fairly unpopular ruler by this point. The Tsarina, Grand Duchess Alexandra, was a German princess, which when you're in the middle of a massive war with Germany isn't a recipe for popularity. Further, the heir to the throne was born with hemophilia, and the royal family eventually turned to an illiterate Siberian mystic, **Grigori Rasputin**, to use his "magic powers" to heal the prince. The creepy and self-involved mystic used his influence to gain wealth and power, and was deeply unpopular with everyone not named Romanov.

The Tsar had also made the mistake of personally becoming commander-in-chief of the Russian war effort in September 1915, following the German conquest of Poland, and so became personally associated with the massive Russian defeats of the war.

A bread riot in St. Petersburg in 1917 blew up once police started firing on the crowds, and the rag-tag conscript regiments still near the city mutinied rather than put down the riots by force. Unrest turned into revolution, the **February Revolution**, and the Tsar abdicated. A democratic government took power under **Alexandr Kerensky**, but his provisional government decided to continue the war. The 1917 **Kerensky Offensive**, meant to prove to the Western Allies that Russia remained an important partner, was a miserable failure, and continued supply problems for the cities meant that unrest continued to grow.

Vladimir Lenin, the leading figure of the Bolshevik faction of the Russian Socialist Party, sought to use that continued unrest to engineer a second revolution, in which the workers' **Soviets** (the Russian word for council) and their militias (the **Red Guard**) overthrew the Kerensky government and seized power. This **October Revolution** is perhaps better understood as a coup than a popular uprising, in which the radical Bolsheviks replaced the moderate Mensheviks and non-socialist democrats of Kerensky's government. The Bolshevik motto was simple: **Bread and Peace!**

Did You Know?

Lenin had actually spent most of the war in exile in Switzerland for fear of the Tsar's secret police. After the February Revolution, he made a secret deal with the German government for transport to Russia via Finland. The Germans hoped that Lenin would destabilize the country and lead to Russia exiting the war.

After seizing the capital, the new Bolshevik government sought an immediate peace deal with the German government, leading to Russian capitulation and the **Treaty of Brest-Litovsk**. Russia got peace but lost a third of European Russia to German control. However, the Bolsheviks got the space to turn their attention to winning the **Russian Civil War**, which would last until 1922.

Mensheviks vs. Bolsheviks 🕛	
Mensheviks	**Bolsheviks**
• Moderate Socialists	• Radical Communists
• Supported Kerensky's government	• Opposed Kerensky's government
• Opposed total government control of the economy	• Imposed total government control of the economy

Yankee Doodle Dandy 💬

On the Western Front, the Russian surrender allowed the German military to transfer millions of men from the Eastern Front for one last attempt to smash the Allied lines. In the meantime, however, the United States had declared war on Germany, in April 1917, following a series of submarine attacks on British and American shipping vessels (most famously the *Lusitania*, a passenger ship being used to transport munitions). The US military was originally very small, but grew rapidly. By the time the big German attack came (**Operation Michael**) in March 1918, over 300,000 American troops had arrived in France and another million were training and readying to embark. This brought the

French and British enough reinforcements to withstand the German on-slaught. After the failure of Operation Michael, the Germans had no way to replace their lost soldiers, while millions of U.S. troops sailed to France to replace the Allies' losses. Eventually U.S. numbers and the deployment of a multitude of primitive tanks, along with the collapse of German morale, managed to drive the Germans out of France and then Belgium in late 1918. The Imperial German government signed an armistice in November 1918, ending the war.

The last year of the war also saw one of the biggest pandemic outbreaks in modern history. Starting in January of 1918, a strain of influenza (the spanish flu) broke out and spread like wildfire, with roughly 500 million people falling ill and 50 to a 100 million people dying—three to five percent of the world's population! The dislocation and immiseration caused by the war were likely contributing factors to the severity of the outbreak.

 Did You Know?

The Spanish flu didn't originate in Spain! It only gained that name because Spain was the only country during World War I to remain neutral...and could therefore freely report on the pandemic! Other European countries attempted to shut down news of the spread of the virus.

Drawing Lines on Maps

The Paris Peace Conference met in Versailles in January 1919 to negotiate a peace treaty. The Germans basically had to take what they were given, and Austria-Hungary had collapsed and disappeared, so the negotiations were mostly between the United States, France, and Britain. Woodrow Wilson, the U.S. president, wanted a just and equal peace that would help prevent future wars, along with the establishment of a League of Nations to arbitrate disputes. France had taken the brunt of the war and wanted Germany to pay through the nose and then disappear. Britain was somewhere in the middle. German payments were super important for France and Britain since the war had been very,

very expensive. In 1913 dollars, the Allies spent roughly $147 billion on the war while the Central Powers spent about $61 billion. For some sense of scale, in 2018 dollars that's $3.7 trillion and $1.5 trillion dollars respectively.

When thinking about the cost of the war, you shoud remember how very many people died. Approximately 6 million civilians on both sides died of disease, hunger, displacement, or military action, while approximately 11 million soldiers died during the war with the Allies losing over 6 million and the Central Powers over 4 million. Another 23 million were wounded.

Though Wilson did get his League of Nations, France got most of what it wanted, including a demilitarized Germany (limited to an army of only 100,000 men) without an air force, submarines, or tanks; enormous amounts of money in reparations; and the return of the two provinces of Alsace and Lorraine, lost to Germany after the Franco-Prussian War. The treaty justified sticking Germany with the bill for the war (Germany was forced to pay $31.4 billion dollars in reparations, the equivalent of $442 billion dollars today) by asserting that Germany was completely at fault for the war in **Article 231**, the war guilt clause. Other treaties created a number of new nation-states in Eastern Europe, including Czechoslovakia, Hungary, Romania, Yugoslavia, Poland, Lithuania, Latvia, Estonia, and Finland. The Middle East and Africa were also re-divided between the British and the French, creating the **Mandate System**.

 Ask Yourself...

Why was the First World War important? How did it change the trajectory of European history?

The Interwar Period: Weimar Germany ❶

The Imperial German government collapsed soon after signing the armistice, and the Social Democratic opposition spearheaded the creation of the Weimar Republic, a democratic German state. However, the leaders of the republic were forced to sign the Versailles Treaty, which for obvious reasons was hated, and began its rule by endorsing far-right paramilitary groups (the **Freikorps**—basically proto-Nazis) to put down communist uprisings looking to create a Soviet-style state in Germany. The Freikorps eventually tried to take over the state, in the so-called **Kapp Putsch** of 1920, but were stopped by a Socialist-led general strike. So a lot of internal problems.

To make matters worse, the burden of paying the massive reparations demanded under Versailles led to **hyperinflation**, further destabilizing Germany. Hyperinflation occurs when the value of currency decreases rapidly. This inflation was only stopped in October 1923 with the introduction of a new currency, the **Rentenmark**. Eventually, Germany's relationships with the other powers began to normalize, marked by the **Locarno Pact** of 1925, in which Germany agreed to respect France's borders and to keep the Rhine demilitarized. This also allowed for Germany to become part of the League of Nations at last, powerless though the organization was. By the late 1920s, it seemed like things were getting better and the Weimar Republic might just have a chance to survive.

In early 1922, about 320 Marks (the German currency) were worth one dollar. In November 1923, you would need more than 4 trillion Marks to buy a dollar. The whole country's savings and investments became worthless almost overnight.

Red AND Dead ❗

The Russian Civil War, fought between the Reds (the Bolshevik forces, mostly based in the cities) and the Whites (monarchists, conservatives, and republicans mostly based in the rural areas), cost almost 10 million lives before ending in a Communist victory. Once over, Lenin inaugurated what he called the **New Economic Policy**, or NEP, which used limited market mechanisms to encourage Russians to rebuild their shattered economy. However, the General Secretary, **Joseph Stalin**, had different ideas. Once Lenin died and Stalin took over, he ended the NEP, eliminated private property, purged his enemies, and forced the collectivization of Soviet agriculture. In the process, the Soviet state murdered all of his opponents, including the wealthier peasants, or **Kulaks**. Using forced labor and government control of resources, he focused on building up heavy industrial capacity through **Five-Year Plans** setting out the government's goals for economic progress. Coal, steel, concrete—these were what Stalin cared about. That, and using the international socialist movement as tools of Soviet policy. The **Third International**, or **Comintern**, was a world-wide organization meant to advance socialism, as the two internationals before it, but now the Soviet Union, as the first and only Communist state in the world, dominated the International and used it as a way of employing leftist movements abroad as tools of Soviet foreign policy.

An Arts Explosion

The Interwar Period was neither stable nor secure, but it did produce some very interesting creations. One such was **Dadaism**, an arts movement that embedded the collapse of the orderly, liberal, progressive prewar Europe into abstraction, surrealism, and meaninglessness.

Cut With the Dada Kitchen Knife Through the Last Weimar Beer-Belly Cultural Epoch in Germany by Hannah Höch

In the Soviet Union, **Soviet Realism** revolutionized the art world, focusing on idealized political themes such as glorious workers, larger-than-life soldiers, and peasants and workers heroically building the future.

Pioneer Girl with Book by Nikolay Kasatkin

Bankruptcy as a Way of Life

The late 1920s were a reasonably good time—reparations had ended in Germany, the stock market was booming across the United States and Europe, and it seemed like things were going well. Unfortunately, most of this was built on stock speculation based on nothing much, and in 1929, the stock market crashed, wiping out enormous amounts of paper wealth. As a partial consequence, everybody panicked about whether or not banks were sound, and tried to withdraw their money immediately. Too many people withdrawing their deposits caused banks to collapse, which made more people panic, which made more banks collapse. This also caused U.S. banks to call in their loans to European institutions, which spread the panic to Europe with the collapse of the Austrian **Credit-Anstalt** bank in 1931.

So how did the bank collapse end up causing the **Great Depression**? This requires a brief digression into economics. The loss of private wealth from the stock market crash and bank failures reduced private spending—businesses and consumers bought less stuff. This reduced economic activity as well as tax receipts for governments. Western governments at the time were committed to maintaining the **Gold Standard**, which was the idea that all of the money a government could spend was limited to the amount of gold it happened to have lying around. So if taxes fell, there was only so much money they could afford to spend, and when private spending collapsed soon after, government spending also fell. This further reduced the amount of stuff being bought, so economic activity fell further, so the government spent less, and so on until they've lost 40 percent of your GDP.

One man, **John Maynard Keynes**, thought this was ridiculous. He argued that reduced private spending could be compensated for by increased government spending to prevent recessions and depressions, and that governments were not, in fact, limited by how much gold they had lying around but could borrow and print money if needed to create economic demand. The United States under President Franklin Roosevelt left the gold standard early and spent enormous amounts of money, leading to rapid recovery. On the other hand, Weimar Germany under Chancellor **Heinrich Brüning** kept cutting and cutting government spending, and the German economy collapsed. Looks like Keynes had a point.

A Bundle of Sticks ❗

 ### *Did You Know?*

"Fascism" comes from the Latin word "fasces," which is represented by an axe bound together by a bunch of sticks! It was a symbol of strength via unity. [No individualists wanted!]

The consequences of the Great Depression in Europe did much to empower radical ideologies such as Fascism and Communism and to discredit liberal democracy. But what exactly *is* Fascism? Fascism as an ideology, like communism, is generally opposed to the individual.

Unlike Communism, which is interested in economic class and argues that everyone is equal, Fascism is interested in the nation, the folk, the people, understood as a group bound by **blood and soil**. Fascism believes in hierarchies, where the strong rule the weak, and strong peoples rule weak peoples. Typically, Fascism is implemented by a singular leader who is thought to embody the virtues and strengths of the people. Economically, Fascism is marked by **corporatism**, or the cooperation of big business with the state and the elimination of workers' movements. Fascists hate democracy and love dictatorships.

Il Duce 🔋

Fascism originated in Italy, named by the founder of the National Fascist Party, **Benito Mussolini**. In Italy, Fascism got its appeal from the disasters Italy suffered in the First World War, and Mussolini came to power more or less legally after an intimidation campaign culminating in the 1922 **March on Rome**. He wasn't very effective at taking over the country, though; King Victor Emmanuel III remained on the throne and Mussolini came to an agreement with the Pope, in what was called the **Lateran Pacts**. Il Duce, Italian for "the leader," was a monster, but something of a pathetic one.

Virulent Fascism 🔋

German Fascism is tightly bound up with the figure of **Adolf Hitler**. An Austrian who moved to Bavaria to avoid conscription but fought for Germany in World War I, he ended the war in a hospital after surviving a gas attack. He ended up joining and then taking over the German Workers' Party, renaming it the **National Socialist German Workers' Party**, or Nazi Party for short. He was a compelling speaker who hated Jews, Communists, democrats, and a host of others, and in 1923 he sought to take over the Bavarian state government in what was called the **Beer Hall Putsch**. Unfortunately for him, the march was suppressed by the state police, and Hitler was sent to prison. While there, he wrote *Mein Kampf* (My Struggle), a screed which laid out his eventual program. Released from prison under a general amnesty, he went back to political organizing. Despite his gifts as a rabble-rouser, Hitler didn't gain much traction until the Great Depression. The 1930 and 1932 elections, called as the Center Party government under Heinrich Brüning continued to double down on austerity measures, gave 102 and then 196 seats out of 608 total to the Nazis. Once Hitler had a majority in Parliament, the conservative German President, Paul von Hindenburg, chose to offer him the Chancellorship and he was sworn in in 1933.

Though this was the high water mark of popular electoral success for the Nazis, Hitler used a fire in the Reichstag, the German Parliament building, to push a law called the **Enabling Act** into power. Though it remains unclear who set the fire, Hitler blamed Communists and the German Parliament voted to grant him emergency powers. Using the Enabling Act, Hitler established a dictatorship (totally legally) and set about crushing other independent groups with some degree of political power. The biggest one left was the army, and they were very worried about the *Sturmabteilung*, or SA. The SA was the Nazi paramilitary arm, previously responsible for such things as murdering Communists and voter intimidation, and the army wanted to be the only source of armed men. Hitler thus kicked off what we call the **Night of the Long Knives** in 1934, during which he had all of the SA leaders assassinated—including his longtime friend Ernst Röhm. All young people were required to join the Nazi youth movement, appropriately named the **Hitler Youth**, and Hitler empowered **Joseph Goebbels** as his propaganda minister to smear opponents and support his regime.

Decadent Democracies 🚹

While all of this was happening, the Western democracies that had won the First World War stood by in varying degrees of horror, irritation, or indifference. For Great Britain, winning the war was great and all, but it was so very expensive that for many Britons it didn't feel much different from losing. **David Lloyd-George**, the Liberal Party prime minister who won the war and negotiated the peace, had promised that postwar Britain would be "a land fit for heroes," but the actual outcome was a reduction in the standard of living for most Britons. Unemployment was high, wages were stagnant, and housing quality was dropping. There was widespread feeling that the war wasn't worth it, and thus widespread opposition to another war. His problems were compounded by the 1918 **Representation of the People Act**, which extended the franchise to all adult men and women over the age of 30, tripling the size of the electorate. The result was the collapse of the Liberal Party and its replacement with the social-democratic Labour Party—in the 1923 elections Lloyd-George was replaced by **Ramsay MacDonald**, the first Labour Prime Minister. The Great Depression crippled Labour rule, however, and Conservatives achieved a majority in parliament beginning in 1931.

Though the early postwar years were marked by economic growth and French assertiveness in Europe, French politics were hard-hit by the Great Depression, which strengthened radical right and radical left parties. French Fascists were greatly encouraged by Hitler's rise, and in response the center-left and left parties in France, including the Communists, formed a **Popular Front** in 1936. This meant that they pledged to all work together and cooperate in forming a government in order to prevent a Fascist government, and they succeeded! In the 1936 elections, the Popular Front won 386 out of 608 seats and formed a Socialist-dominated government. The new government had run on a series of labor and welfare programs, including legalizing strikes and collective bargaining, mandating 12 days of paid leave yearly, limiting the standard work week to 40 hours, and raising wages. This legislative package, known as the **Matignon Accords,** was passed rapidly.

This early success was unfortunately not a sign that the government was stable and unified. The outbreak of the **Spanish Civil War** in 1936 split the government. The Prime Minister, **Léon Blum**, was deeply opposed to Fascism (in 1935, the French Fascist group **Action Francaise** had sent a goon squad after the Jewish politician that almost beat him to death), but feared that supporting the Spanish Republicans would split the government or even lead to civil war in France. The best the French could do was to declare a policy of non-intervention as they sought to build up their military to face the German threat.

La Guerra 🚨

A shaky Spanish democracy, established only in 1931 after the collapse of the Spanish monarchy, faced the same European-wide threats as France and Britain with much less popular commitment to democratic norms. Though socialists narrowly won the 1936 elections, much of the Spanish Army, under the leadership of General **Francisco Franco**, mutinied and seized control of much of Spain. However, republican loyalists organized a defense of Spanish democracy in opposition to Franco's coup and the situation spiraled into a brutal civil war, one with foreign aid coming in for both sides. For example, much of the German Air Force got its training bombing and strafing Spanish Republican military and civilian targets, such as the terror bombing of **Guernica**. The Republicans were largely abandoned by the Western allies, and resorted to the Soviet Union for supplies. Eventually, though, Italian and German support and weapons crushed the Republicans, and they lost in 1939. Franco ended up as the dictator of a Fascist Spain, though one with the good sense to stay out of World War II.

The Dreaded Onset of World War II 🚨

The causes of the Second World War were much more straightforward than those of the First. Once in power, Hitler moved to overthrow the Versailles Treaty. In 1935, he began rearming Germany, to no response. The next year, he remilitarized the Rhine and signed a treaty with Mussolini, creating the **Rome-Berlin Axis**, which expanded in 1937 to include Imperial Japan. In neither case did France or Britain respond. This convinced Hitler that he could get away with anything, so he moved on to annexing Austria in 1938, in what is called the **Anschluss**. His threat to annex the **Sudetenland**, the western region of Czechoslovakia, though, led to a summit in which France and Britain agreed to allow Hitler to seize the Sudetenland in exchange for not annexing the rest of the country. The British Prime Minister, **Neville Chamberlain**, claimed that this Munich Agreement would lead to "peace in our time." This was a policy of **appeasement**—give Hitler what he wanted, the thinking went, and he'll calm down and shape up. The next year, Hitler tossed the agreement in the garbage and annexed the rest of Czechoslovakia. Next up was Poland, but Chamberlain and Edouard Daladier, the French prime minister, knew they'd been played for fools and threatened war if

Hitler invaded Poland. Hitler didn't take this very seriously—why would he, at this point?—and, in cahoots with the Soviet Union, invaded Poland on September 1, 1939, beginning the Second World War.

Why was Hitler cooperating with the Soviet Union, considering he hated Communists so much? Well the **Molotov-Ribbentrop Pact** (named after the two foreign ministers who signed it) was essentially both sides saying we don't want to fight *yet*, so let's destroy a mutual enemy.

 Ask Yourself...
Was the Second World War inevitable? Why or why not?

World War II 🔊

The conflict began with an attack on **Poland** in September 1939. The Germans used a new technique called the *blitzkrieg*, which were swift ground attacks supported by jets overhead. The Poles fell in a month, and Europe fell into that winter with little to no fighting, known as the **Phony War**.

The next summer, Germany moved swiftly to the west and invaded France, defeating that nation in just six weeks. This is known as the **fall of France**. It occurred partially because they'd built **the Maginot Line**, a series of tough defenses, but the Germans simply walked around them and encircled the French armies. As a result of the fall of France, the British quickly staged a heroic retreat from the Belgian beaches at **Dunkirk.***

---

*See the movie *Dunkirk*. It has Harry Styles, whom we're told is a very good singer.

Did You Know?

Germany invaded France three times in 70 years (1870, 1914, and 1940).

Blame followed, and soon the French had formed a new government—
Vichy France, under the elderly **Marshal Philippe Pétain**, using the
opportunity to create a more authoritarian French government. Many
from the last administration went into exile in London, including a charismatic general named **Charles de Gaulle**. The Vichy government called
him a traitor as the French people began to assist the Germans with the
deportation of Jews.*

Next, Hitler set his sights on England, waging the extraordinary **Battle
of Britain**, bombing London night and day via the **Luftwaffe**, the German
air force. England had a new extraordinary leader in **Winston Churchill**,
who inspired his nation to survive through a series of brilliant radio
addresses. To be fair, England had a couple of advantages that the
Germans did not—**radar** and **codebreakers**.** The **Royal Air Force** was
given a break when Germany stopped bombing air bases and turned
to the cities instead. In the end, Hitler gave up, and turned toward the
Soviet Union.

The Holocaust, the slaughter of six million Jews, did not begin sud-
denly. Soon after taking power, the Nazis implemented the **Nuremberg
Laws,** depriving Jews of citizenship and forcing them to wear a yellow
Star of David on their clothing. Many Jews left Germany at that point,
though many stayed. The oppression grew worse, and in 1938, the
Nazis launched **Kristallnacht**, the "night of broken glass."

❗ The Nazis were quite obsessed with what they euphemistically
called the **Jewish Question**. The obsession grew so large that they
decided to solve the question with something they called the **Final
Solution**, which meant large-scale extermination of Jews. They decided
to do this in Poland, since it had the largest concentration of Jews in
the world directly under German control. Initially, the murders were

---

*Self-awareness level: zero.

**See the movie *The Imitation Game*. It stars Benedict Cumberbatch, who sometimes looks like an otter.
(No, really. Google it.)

committed in mobile vans, or Jews were machine-gunned in the streets. Soon, however, seeking more efficiency, they opened the infamous system of concentration camps, the most notorious of these being **Auschwitz**. At the camps, the prisoners were sorted according to who could work and who would die. The notorious **Josef Mengele** also selected certain prisoners to perform gruesome experiments upon, particularly twins. Besides Jews, the camps also contained "gypsies" (or Roma as they prefer to be called), homosexuals, Jehovah's Witnesses, Russian prisoners of war, Communists, and others considered by the Nazis to be "undesirables." About 7 million people were slaughtered, 6 million of whom were Jews.

Things changed in 1941 for two reasons. One, the United States entered the war, sparking hope and providing much-needed material assistance. Two, Germany invaded the Soviet Union. For the Nazis, this opened up a war on two fronts—the Allied forces to the west and the Soviets to the east—which sealed their eventual fate.

Complicating matters even further, the Germans also had to assist the Italians in North Africa, who were desperately trying to push the British out of Egypt. So that's actually a war on *three* fronts.

❗ By late 1943, the **Allies** met in Tehran and decided to stage an invasion of western Europe from Great Britain the following year. This became the infamous **D-Day** invasion, which was brutal and bloody, but successful.* The Allies gained a beachhead in northwest France and began to slowly work their way across the continent toward Berlin.

You already know how this massive war eventually ended—the good guys won.** But what you may not know is that over 50 million people died in World War II, mostly civilians. You also may not understand the massive cleanup that was involved. Germany had to undergo a process of **denazification**, which included the Nuremberg Trials. This was a series of trials in which Nazi officials were charged with **crimes against humanity**. Several were punished, and two committed suicide in their cells. Germany calls this lowest moment of their national history the **Zero Hour**, which should explain itself.

---

*See the movie *Saving Private Ryan*. It stars Tom Hanks, who will be the first to tell you that there's no crying in baseball.

**If they hadn't, you'd be reading this book in German.

Ask Yourself...

If the United States had never entered World War II, could the Russians eventually have defeated the Nazi menace alone?

❗ After the war, the overriding wish of European and American leaders was to create stability. President Franklin Roosevelt had first envisioned an international body of nations in the **Atlantic Charter** (1941), and in 1945 his successor and European leaders finally acted upon it by forming the **United Nations**. It was intended to stabilize the world. To that same end, **new democratic governments** began to pop up across Europe, ones that offered their citizens full rights and social welfare programs in return for giving up radical demands.

This is not to say that everything was peaches and cream. There were still small ethnic disruptions in the decades following the war—the **Basque** were still agitating in Spain, the nationalists in Ireland and Chechnya. But overall, Western Europe was trying, and succeeding, in building something new after the self-imposed devastation.

At this time, **the role of women** in Western Europe changed, improving substantially. Second-wave feminism swept across Europe in the 1960s, new family-friendly policies were put in place, and women pursued professional careers in record numbers. In politics, a new generation of female political leaders was arriving, including **Margaret Thatcher** in England, **Mary Robinson** in Ireland, and **Edith Cresson** in France.

The Soviet system, however, had a different set of priorities. If Europe is a body, then it was starting to catch a cold. Or, better yet, a **Cold War**.

Three Theories on the Causes of the Cold War

1. For the **Traditionalists** (a position that emerged in the earliest days of the Cold War), the Soviet Union, under the brutal dictatorship of Joseph Stalin, was fundamentally responsible for the development of hostilities between the East and West.

2. Beginning in the 1960s (in part a reflection of the challenges that were being posed to all forms of established authority and anger over the Vietnam War), a new school of Cold War thought, known as revisionism, began to appear. For the **Revisionists,** fear of a postwar economic downturn (as was the case after 1918) meant that, in 1945, the United States was not seeking to make the world safe for democracy but was instead seeking to make it safe for American trade.

3. By the 1980s, a third position began to emerge, that of the **Post-Revisionists**, which perhaps not surprisingly took a middle ground. For the Post-Revisionists, even if the Soviet Union bore the brunt of the responsibility, the United States was more to blame than the Traditionalists might argue.

The strain between the Soviets and the West had been present as far back as the **Yalta Conference** of 1945, which unofficially concluded World War II. Stalin had signaled to Churchill and Roosevelt that, after Hitler was defeated, he intended to keep a presence in Eastern Europe. Soviet troops were already on the ground there, and the United States and the United Kingdom didn't have the energy or willpower to challenge him. And in the zone of eastern Germany that the Soviets supported, they undermined democracy by promoting policies that led to the formation of one-party states.

The West finally contested the growing presence of the Soviets four years later, in 1949, by establishing the **North Atlantic Treaty Organization** (NATO).* The Soviet Union answered by forming a similar treaty among its allies and vassal states. This was the **Warsaw Pact**.

The Soviets soon dominated Central and Eastern Europe, corralling all the old nationalities, bringing them together under a single Soviet net—whether they wanted to be involved or not. The Soviets even called these programs **people's democracies**, since it was presumed that they weren't ready for full communism yet. Stalin saw that the United States was offering financial assistance via the Marshall Plan to any European nation willing to move toward a capitalistic model. So the Soviets moved toward direct control in places like Hungary, intimidating voters. In 1946, Winston Churchill remarked that an "**Iron Curtain** has fallen across the continent," and the phrase stuck.

The End of Imperialism

The beginning of European decolonization took place on August 15, 1947, when India declared independence from the British Empire. Soon the weakened European powers were divesting themselves of colonies as quickly as they could sign the paperwork.

That same year, England announced that it was withdrawing from Palestine. The next year, 1948, a new Jewish homeland, **Israel**, was established over protests from Arab Palestinians, who claimed then and continue to claim the same land.

---

*NATO still exists, even though the Soviets are long gone.

Then in 1956, Great Britain got a nasty surprise from **Egypt**. Though Egypt had been an independent nation since 1922, the British controlled the Suez Canal. President Abdul Nasser announced the nationalization of the Canal, which prompted the British (with France and Israel) to make a surprise attack on Egypt. The American and Soviet governments stepped up to defend Egypt, and Britain slunk back to their island, giving up interest in Egypt.

Soon after, the British began the process of decolonization in sub-Saharan Africa. Ghana broke first, in 1957, followed by Nigeria, Sierra Leone, Uganda, and Kenya. There was resistance in **Rhodesia**, however, as the large number of British settlers formed their own white-supremacist government. By 1980, Africans finally won control over that land, which they renamed Zimbabwe.

The French lost territory as well, nearly breaking into civil war over the question of **Algeria**, which had been a French possession for over a century. Charles de Gaulle settled the question by granting Algeria its independence. This stung twice as hard, since the French had earlier lost control of **Vietnam** to rebel forces led by **Ho Chi Minh**.* As a result, the country was divided into a communist north and an American-led south.

 Did You Know?

A scholar recently calculated that, at one time or another, the British had invaded almost 180 of the 200 nations in the world!

---

*Which is why today the Vietnamese make sandwiches using French baguettes.

The Creation of a European Union ❗

It couldn't have been easy to knit together a shattered continent after the most violent century in human history, but Europe somehow managed to drag itself to its feet and shake hands all around.

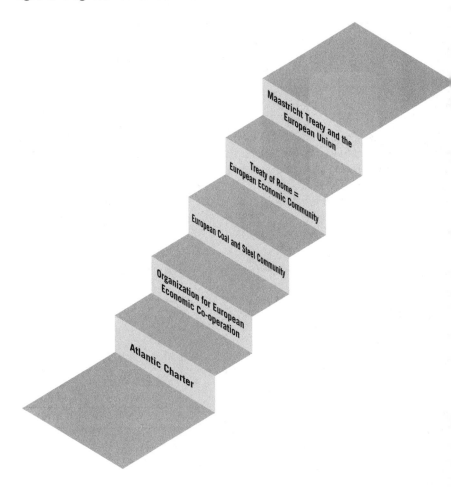

Maastricht Treaty and the European Union

Treaty of Rome = European Economic Community

European Coal and Steel Community

Organization for European Economic Co-operation

Atlantic Charter

! Reunification was a slow-going process—three generations passed before it was accomplished—but each step was viewed as an inevitable one toward economic unification of Europe.

The first vision of a unified Europe was found in the **Atlantic Charter** (1941), an agreement signed by the United States and the United Kingdom (and later others) agreeing to a set of common goals, including the lowering of trade restrictions, global cooperation, freedom of the seas, and the envisioning of what later became the United Nations.

The **Organization for European Economic Co-operation** (OEEC) was created after World War II to properly hand out the dollars that the United States was distributing into Europe via the Marshall Plan. Later, in 1961, it started the process of lowering trade restrictions and changed the name to Organization for Economic Co-operation and Development (OECD).

The **European Coal and Steel Community** (ESCS) (1951) combined French and German coal and steel industries. This was smartly done so that neither one could declare war on the other again. It was kind of like being handcuffed to your bully.

In 1957, the members of the ECSC signed the **Treaty of Rome**, which established the **European Economic Community** (EEC). These members (later joined by Britain, Ireland, and Denmark) lifted almost all trade restrictions among member states. Much later, in 1986, an adjustment provided for the free movement of capital, labor, and services.

Finally, the **Maastricht Treaty** of 1992 established everybody's dream—a common currency. Called the Euro, it didn't go into circulation until 10 years later. It wasn't universally accepted, though. The United Kingdom, though part of the EEC, refused to give up its beloved pound sterling. It also changed the name from the EEC to the **European Union** (EU).

Post-WWII Developments in Western European States

England

After the war ended, Winston Churchill and the Conservative party were booted out of power, replaced by the **Labour Party** and **Clement Attlee**. A series of liberal reforms were undertaken by Sir **William Beveridge**, culminating in the establishment of a cradle-to-grave social welfare program—the highlight being the establishment of the **National Health Service** (NHS), which provided a comprehensive system of free health care. The Labour Party also **nationalized industries**, including the Bank of England, railroads, and the electric, iron, and steel industries. Still, it was a dark economic time for many decades, an era now known as the **Age of Austerity.** England was a major debtor to the United States, and it was essentially broke. It still spent on military commitments overseas, and it had to play defense in the Cold War that had started to loom.

 ## Did You Know?

England was still rationing butter and sugar almost 10 years after
World War II ended!

The war did have one lovely side effect: British politics grew quite friendly. When the conservatives came back into power, for instance, they didn't sweep aside the advances made by liberals. Other than reversing the nationalization of the iron and steel industries, they actually supported the social welfare programs of the Labour party. This has come to be known as the **Politics of Consensus**. Both parties agreed that government should play a larger role in society.

Overall, however, Britain declined economically after the war. The reasons:

- Older factories that weren't being modernized (see Germany)
- Lack of central economic planning (see France)
- Powerful unions that forced higher wages

Just as Churchill had done, it would take the arrival of a new figurehead to pull the United Kingdom out of its doldrums. **Margaret Thatcher**, England's first female prime minister, was that figure. She took tight control over the money supply, reduced inflation, made sharp cuts in public spending, reduced unions, and cut taxes, particularly for higher earners.

She was surprisingly unpopular, and her career survived only because of the boost in popularity following the successful war that Britain fought with Argentina in 1982 over the "tiny and worthess" Falkland Islands. She eventually resigned and was replaced by **John Major**, who continued all of her policies except one—he signed the Maastricht Treaty, bringing England into the EU.

"The Falklands thing was a fight between two bald men over a comb."

—Jorge Luis Borges

France ❗

Sadly, France hadn't put up much resistance to Germany during the war; many had collaborated. This meant a period of national reckoning afterward, as the French had to face their own sorrowful role in deporting 66,000 Jews to Germany. At this time, the people established the **Fourth Republic**.

Charles de Gaulle had been the leader of the French government-in-exile during the war. However, he stepped away from politics when the Fourth Republic refused to establish a strong presidency. The Fourth Republic then tussled with a series of colonial problems, including the disastrous defeat in Indochina in 1954 and a revolt that broke out in Algeria the same year.

The crisis in Algeria brought de Gaulle back to politics, and he led the vote for a plebiscite in 1958 establishing the **Fifth Republic**, which created a more powerful presidency. He won the office, and he quickly committed himself to restoring France to a leading place on the global stage. To maintain self-defense, he refused to sign the **Limited Test Ban Treaty**—then exploded France's first hydrogen bomb in 1968.

"How can you govern a country which has two hundred and forty-six varieties of cheese?"

—Charles de Gaulle

France's economy was the exact opposite of England's—it was booming by the 1950s and 1960s. Part of this could perhaps be due to the fact that Communists had been pushed out of French national politics by American demand. Or perhaps it could be explained by the **Monnet Plan**, an economic program designed by **Jean Monnet**, who provided for nonpolitical technocrats to run the economy. This increased foreign investment. Together with central planning, the French economy sky-rocketed, and life was transformed in France as the people flocked to stores to buy cars, televisions, and dishwashers. This became known as **Americanization**, and it really hasn't stopped since.

 Did You Know?

The *Académie Française* has been trying to preserve the French language by attempting to ban foreign words such as *blog, hashtag, parking, email,* and *weekend!*

Italy

Like France, Italy's productivity exploded in the 1950s and 1960s, to the point that it was referred to as the **economic miracle**. This was achieved by the Institute for Industrial Reconstruction (IRI), a fascist organization that was the conduit by which the national government controlled shipbuilding, airlines, metallurgy, and the chemical industry. Over six million southern Italians moved to the north at this time, providing cheap labor supply.

In fact, the extreme poverty of southern Italy, known as the **southern question**, was a top priority, since many of Mussolini's political opponents had been exiled to the south and now were talking about it. They broke up the large feudal-style estates via land reform, and then pumped money into the region through a series of five-year plans. But there still remains a significant economic gap between the industrialized north and the agricultural south.

By the 1970s, economic problems were increasing, including high unemployment, inflation, and the loss of a staggering number of workdays to strikes. This caused a rise in political terrorism from the left, culminating in 1978 when the **Red Brigades** kidnapped former Prime Minster Aldo Moro and eventually murdered him when the government refused to negotiate his release.

Germany ❗

After the war concluded, Germany was devastated. Its main city, Berlin, was divided into four occupation zones: American, British, French, and Soviet. When the United States and Britain introduced a new currency into their occupation zones without seeking Soviet approval, Stalin retaliated by completely cutting off the city from the west. So the United States began to send supplies by air to its besieged people. The **Berlin Airlift** went on for 10 and a half months. As a result of the airlift, France, England, and the United States decided to pool their zones, and created the **Federal Republic of Germany**, better known as West Germany. Stalin then declared his portion to be the **German Democratic Republic**, better known as East Germany. In 1961, the East German border police began solemnly building a concrete barrier down the middle of the city of Berlin. This eventually became known as the **Berlin Wall**, and one of its purposes was to keep East German scientists (and other intellectuals) from escaping to the West. It remained standing for almost 30 years.

The early years of West Germany were dominated by **Konrad Adenauer**, the head of the **Christian Democratic Union** party. He was an anti-Nazi German conservative who ushered in a period of enormous economic growth, just as France and Italy experienced. The economy quadrupled in just over 10 years. Granted, West Germany was aided by "brain drain"—educated Eastern Europeans immigrating to West Germany as they fled the Soviet system. But the prosperity went to everybody—as in France, workers experienced increased wages from higher productivity, which they used to buy cars, dishwashers, jeans, and so on. The government official responsible for this economic boom was **Ludwig Erhard**, the minister of economics who became chancellor following Adenauer's retirement in 1961.

During this time, the other political party, the **Social Democrats**, were struggling. To rebrand themselves, the Social Democrats stopped talking about class struggle, and then elevated the charismatic **Willy Brandt** as the leader. When he became chancellor in 1969, he reached out to the Soviets and their satellite states in Eastern Europe. This policy, known as **Ostpolitik**, led to the signing of various treaties with the Soviet Union and its satellite states. Fifteen years after he left office, in 1990, another chancellor, **Helmut Kohl**, brought about German reunification. He also was instrumental in the signing of the Maastricht Treaty, which created the European Union.

Collapse of the Communist Bloc ❗

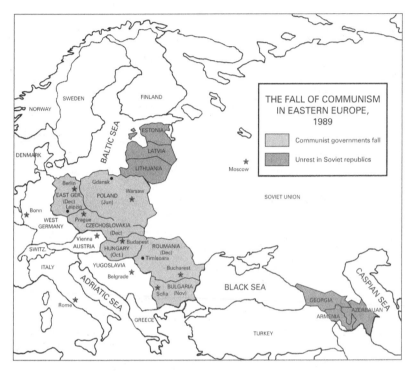

The Fall of Communism in Eastern Europe

For Central and Eastern European states, joining the Soviet Union was a bit like joining the Mafia—once you get in, you can never get out. For example, in 1956, **Hungary** attempted to withdraw from the Soviet system and start a program of liberalization. The Soviets crushed the movement, killing thousands.

Inside the Soviet Union, a power struggle ensued with the death of Stalin. The winner was **Nikita Khruschev**, who refused to execute his opponents (for a nice change) but did deliver a speech in which he smashed his shoe upon the podium while denouncing the United States.

A few years later, in 1968, the people of Czechoslovakia tried to rise up against the Soviets (in the same way that Hungary had earlier), birthing a reform movement known as the **Prague Spring**. The new general secretary of the Soviet Union, **Leonid Brezhnev**, crushed that one too.

By the early 1980s, however, the cracks were starting to show in the Soviet system. The first nation to rebel—and get away with it, kind of— was **Poland**. A movement called **Solidarity**, led by an electrician named **Lech Wałęsa**, demanded the right to form independent trade unions. Later, his movement demanded multiparty elections, and the government was so weak that it agreed. The Communists lost every race.

The cracks spread quickly through the Soviet satellite states. The new Soviet general secretary, **Mikhail Gorbachev**, saw the writing on the wall and worked for a speedy, clean dismantling of the Soviet system. The only exception was **Nicolae Ceaușescu** of Romania, who tried to hold onto power. He and his wife were executed by firing squad.

Russian words to know!

glasnost: openness in debate

perestroika: economic restructuring

The Berlin Wall was torn down not long after, and soon the disintegration was happening faster than Gorbachev (who remained a Communist) had wanted. A failed coup by hardline communists led to the elevation of his rival, **Boris Yeltsin**, who personally led the resistance. By 1991, the Soviet Union had dissolved.

Yeltsin, now the president of the new **Russian Federation**, spent the 1990s introducing free-market capitalism to his country. However, that often translated into no-bid sales of state assets such as utilities to oligarchs, who grew into mammoth power and wealth. Thus was created the Russian Mafia, whose criminal organizations grew enormous. Yeltsin himself seemed to have little consideration for democracy, forcing a new constitution that granted his office expanded powers.

The 1990s also saw severe ethnic warfare and civil war in the former nation of **Yugoslavia**. In short, Muslims and Croats living in the province of Bosnia wanted to form their own nation. However, Serbs living in that same province didn't want to become a minority, and with the help from the president of Yugoslavia, **Slobodan Milošević,** they began "ethnic cleansing," which is code for slaughter. Milošević's later support of a Serbian attack on the province of **Kosovo** led to NATO bombing Serbia for 74 straight days. After the conflict ended—and Yugoslavia split into seven parts—Milošević was turned over to the **International Criminal Tribunal for the former Yugoslavia** by the next president in return for assistance from the West.

Europe Now

Currently Europe is in the midst of a struggle between two opposing forces, each trying to define the continent's identity for the 21st century. On one side, right wing parties have found political success running on nationalist, anti-immigrant sentiment.

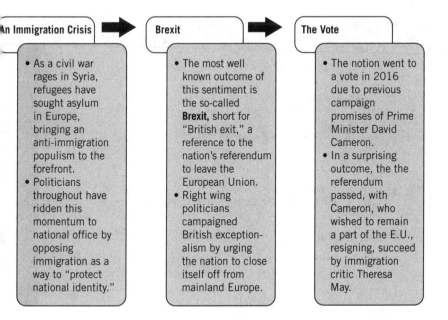

An Immigration Crisis

- As a civil war rages in Syria, refugees have sought asylum in Europe, bringing an anti-immigration populism to the forefront.
- Politicians throughout have ridden this momentum to national office by opposing immigration as a way to "protect national identity."

Brexit

- The most well known outcome of this sentiment is the so-called **Brexit,** short for "British exit," a reference to the nation's referendum to leave the European Union.
- Right wing politicians campaigned British exceptionalism by urging the nation to close itself off from mainland Europe.

The Vote

- The notion went to a vote in 2016 due to previous campaign promises of Prime Minister David Cameron.
- In a surprising outcome, the the referendum passed, with Cameron, who wished to remain a part of the E.U., resigning, succeed by immigration critic Theresa May.

On the other side, Europe's liberals have aimed to uphold the democratic institutions and political and economic alliances that have grown since the years immediately following World War II.

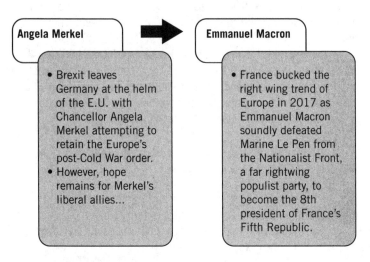

Angela Merkel

- Brexit leaves Germany at the helm of the E.U. with Chancellor Angela Merkel attempting to retain the Europe's post-Cold War order.
- However, hope remains for Merkel's liberal allies...

Emmanuel Macron

- France bucked the right wing trend of Europe in 2017 as Emmanuel Macron soundly defeated Marine Le Pen from the Nationalist Front, a far rightwing populist party, to become the 8th president of France's Fifth Republic.

Year(s)	Event
1914	Assassination of Franz Ferninand (June 28)
1914	Austria-Hungary issues ultimatum to Serbia (July 23)
1914	Austria-Hungary declares war on Serbia (July 28)
1914	Russia begins mobilization (July 29)
1914	Germany declares war on Russia (August 1)
1914	Germany declares war on France (August 3)
1914	Germans defeat Russians at Tannenberg (August 26–30)
1914	First Battle of the Marne (September 5–10)

Year(s)	Event
1914	Completion of the Panama Canal
1915	Gallipoli campaign begins (April 25)
1915	Sinking of the *Lusitania* (May 7)
1915	Germans begin attack on Verdun (February 21)
1916	British launch attack at the Somme (July 1)
1917	Zimmermann Telegram (January 19)
1917	Germany resumes unrestricted submarine warfare (February 1)
1917	Bolsheviks sign armistice with Germany (December 3)
1917	United States declares war on Germany (April 6)
1917	Provisional Government established in Russia (February)
1917	Bolshevik seizure of power (November)
1918	Worldwide influenza outbreak
1918	Female suffrage begins in Great Britain
1918	Germany Republic established after abdication of Kaiser Wilhelm II (November 10)
1918	Armistice brings the war to a close
1919	Treaty of Versailles
1919	Mussolini organizes first Fascist party
1919	Weimar Constitution established

Year(s)	Event
1920	Formation of Communist International
1922	Mussolini becomes Prime Minister of Italy
1923	German hyperinflation
1923	Beer Hall Putsch
1924	Death of Lenin
1924	Dawes Plan
1925	Treaty of Lucarno
1928	First Soviet Five-Year Plan
1929	Beginning of collectivized farms in Soviet Union
1929	Lateran Accord between Mussolini and the Catholic Church
1929	Young Plan
1929	Stock market crash
1930	Nazis make huge electoral gains
1931	Bank failures
1932	Hindenburg defeats Hitler for the German presidency
1932	Nazis become largest party in Reichstag
1933	Hitler becomes chancellor
1933	Reichstag fire

Year(s)	Event
1933	Enabling Act
1933	Germany withdraws from League of Nations
1933	German boycott of Jewish businesses
1934	Beginning of the Great Terror in the Soviet Union
1934	"Night of the Long Knives"
1934	Hitler becomes führer after death of Hindenburg
1935	Germany openly begins rearmament
1935	Italian invasion of Ethiopia
1935	Nuremberg Laws directed against German Jews
1936	Berlin Olympics
1936	German remilitarization of the Rhineland
1936	Beginning of the Spanish Civil War
1938	Germany absorbs Austria in Anschluss
1938	Munich Agreement leads to dismemberment of Czechoslovakia
1938	*Kristallnacht* (November 9)
1939	Nazi-Soviet nonaggression pact
1939	German invasion of Poland
1939	Britain and France declare war on Germany

Year(s)	Event
1940	Fall of France
1940	Winston Churchill replaces Chamberlain as prime minister
1940	Battle of Britain (July–October)
1940	Germans begin Blitz on British cities (September to May 1941)
1941	Germany launches Operation Barbarossa
1941	Japanese attack on Pearl Harbor
1941	30,000 Jews killed at Babi Yar over two days
1941	Atlantic Charter
1942	German advance stopped at Stalingrad
1942	Battle of Midway (June)
1942	Wansee Conference organizes the Final Solution
1943	Battle of Kursk
1943	Allies land in Italy
1943	Mussolini's government fails
1943	Warsaw ghetto uprising
1944	Percentages Agreement between Churchill and Stalin
1944	D-Day
1944	Germans launch Battle of the Bulge (December 16)

Year(s)	Event
1945	Yalta Conference (February 4–11)
1945	Hitler commits suicide (April 30)
1945	V-E Day (May 8)
1945	Victory of British Labour Party over Conservatives (July)
1945	Potsdam Conference (July 17–August 2)
1945	Atomic bomb dropped on Hiroshima (August 6)
1945	V-J Day (August 14)
1945	United Nations' charter is ratified (October)
1945	Nuremberg Trials for crimes against humanity begin (November)
1946	Establishment of French Fourth Republic
1946	Referendum establishes the Italian Republic
1946	Churchill delivers Iron Curtain speech at Westminster College
1947	George Kennan writes the "Long Telegram"
1947	Truman Doctrine
1947	Introduction of the Marshall Plan
1947	India and Pakistan become independent states
1948	Break between the Soviet Union and Yugoslavia
1948	Establishment of the State of Israel

Year(s)	Event
1948	National Health Service established in Great Britain
1948	Soviet dominance in Eastern Europe solidified
1949	Formation of NATO
1949	Berlin Airlift leads to ending blockade after 11 months
1949	Establishment of the Federal Republic of Germany
1949	Establishment of Democratic Republic of Germany
1951	Establishment of the European Coal and Steel Community
1953	Death of Stalin
1954	French suffer defeat in Indochina
1954	Algerian revolt begins
1955	Establishment of the Warsaw Pact
1956	Soviets send in troops to put down Hungarian uprising
1957	Ghana declares its independence from Great Britain
1957	Signing of the Treaty of Rome establishing the EEC
1958	French plebiscite leads to creation of the Fifth Republic
1961	East Germany begins construction of the wall dividing Berlin
1962	France vetoes Britain's attempt to join the European Community
1962	Cuban missile crisis

Year(s)	Event
1968	Wave of student protests in Europe and the United States
1968	Prague Spring
1969	Willy Brandt becomes German chancellor
1972	Irish Troubles begin with the shooting of 13 Catholic peace marchers on "Bloody Sunday"
1973	Oil crisis
1978	Red Brigades kidnap and murder former Prime Minister Aldo Moro
1978	Papal election of John Paul II
1979	Margaret Thatcher becomes prime minister
1981	Francois Mitterand elected president of France
1985	Mikhail Gorbachev becomes leader of the Soviet Union
1989	End of Communist rule in Eastern Europe
1990	Reunification of Germany
1991	End of Soviet Union Boris Yeltsin elected president of newly created Russian Federation
1992	Maastricht Treaty
1992	Beginning of a series of violent conflicts in the former Yugoslavia
1997	Tony Blair becomes prime minister of Great Britain and Northern Ireland

Year(s)	Event
1999	Vladimir Putin becomes president of Russian Federation
2002	Introduction of the euro
2004	Entry into NATO of former Warsaw Pact nations
2008	Dmitry Medvedev becomes president of Russian Federation (Putin becomes prime minister)
2010	David Cameron becomes prime minister of Great Britain and Northern Ireland
2012	Medvedev and Putin switch positions; Medvedev becomes prime minister and Putin becomes president
2016	Great Britain votes to approve "Brexit;" Theresa May becomes Prime Minister

NOTES

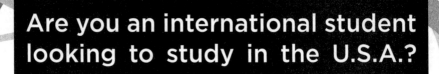

Are you an international student looking to study in the U.S.A.?

Visit us at

https://www.princetonreview.com/global